D0972110

CAPTURE *Her* HEART

Becoming the Godly Husband Your Wife Desires

By Lysa TerKeurst

MOODY PRESS
CHICAGO

© 2002 by
LYSA TERKEURST

All rights reserved. No part of this book may be reproduced in any form without permission in writing from the publisher, except in the case of brief quotations embodied in critical articles or reviews.

All Scripture quotations, unless otherwise indicated, are taken from the *Holy Bible New International Version®*. NIV®. Copyright © 1973, 1978, 1984 by International Bible Society. Used by permission of Zondervan Publishing House. All rights reserved.

Scripture quotations marked *The Message* are from *The Message*. Copyright © by Eugene H. Peterson 1993, 1994, 1995. Used by permission of NavPress Publishing Group.

Editorial services by: Julie-Allyson Ieron, Joy Media

Book design by: Julia Ryan [DesignByJulia]

ISBN: 0-8024-4041-X

1 3 5 7 9 10 8 6 4 2

Printed in the United States of America

CAPTURE *Her* HEART

ACKNOWLEDGMENTS: To Greg, Elsa, Bill, and the rest of the Moody Press staff: Thank you for catching the vision of the project. ■ *To Julie, Mark, and the rest of the Focus on the Family Publishing team: Thank you for helping carry the vision to many.* ■ To Julie-Allyson Ieron: Once again I thank you for lending your editorial expertise. ■ *To Marie Ogram: You are the world's greatest office manager and a wonderful friend. Thank you for all you did to make this project possible!* ■ To other staff members of Proverbs 31 Ministries—Sharon, Joel, Shelly, Sherry, Lisa, Glynnis, Carol, Linda, Miriam, Suzi, Falinda, Ann, and all the many volunteers: I couldn't do what I do without you. What a blessing to work with such first class-people. ■ *To Scott Gordon and team at Promise Keepers: Thank you for all your help surveying and compiling responses in preparation for this project.* ■ To the many couples who allowed me to peek inside your hearts and minds and benefit from the wonderful insights you provided, especially David and Becky, Steve and Sheila, Scott and Melanie, and Angee and Taz. ■ *To all the men and women who have their quotes published within these pages: Thank you and may God richly bless your marriage.*

To the man who has
captured my heart.
I love you, Art,
forever and ever.

*Also dedicated to the men and
women who want their marriages
to be pictures of Christ's grace,
mercy, and love. May these books
help you understand your mate
better and help you fall in love
all over again.*

THE GAME PLAN

Your wife needs you to treat her like a princess.

Your wife needs you to communicate with her.

Your wife needs her friends and needs you to allow her time with the girls, but ultimately she wants you to be her best friend.

Your wife needs you to be a "triple A" encourager by giving her appreciation, affirmation, and admiration.

Your wife needs to feel emotionally filled before she desires to be sexually involved.

Your wife needs you to understand that there are some things you will never understand. This doesn't make either of you right or wrong—just different.

YOU MIGHT NEED THIS BOOK IF . . .

f you have left the toilet seat up nearly drowning your wife during her 2 a.m. trip to the potty.

■ If you have ever been accused of being insensitive because you asked your wife what she did all day.

■ If you have ever expected your wife to go from wiping noses and scrubbing toilets to sex goddess in thirty seconds or less.

■ If your wife has ever asked you that delicate question, "Honey, do I look fat?" and you hesitated for one second . . . or, worse yet, if you said yes.

■ If your wife has ever come home from having her hair done only to hear you say you liked it better before . . . or if you didn't notice her new "do" at all.

■ If you have ever crawled in bed at night with "that something special" on your mind only to have your wife ask you to just hold her, and you've felt frustrated and confused.

■ If you have ever wondered why your wife seemed less than excited to get a new vacuum cleaner or a subscription to *Shape* magazine for her birthday . . . or, worse yet, if you've ever forgotten her birthday.

■ If you have ever been perplexed by your wife's emotional outburst and in an effort to help her you suggested calling an exorcist to help rid her of demons.

■ If you've ever wished you could understand your wife better.

■ If you've ever desired to capture her heart.

If even one of these statements rings true to you, do not pass "Go" and do not collect $200. Go directly to the sales counter, buy this book, and read on.

You do need this book!

Let's face it, most marriages have problems. These problems will lead a couple in one of two directions. They will either lead to building walls that isolate and destroy the relationship or they will lead to creative solutions that strengthen and enhance the relationship.

I believe that within every problem, there is a treasure to be found. I am not writing this book because my husband and I never have problems. Quite the contrary. I am writing this book because we have faced our problems head-on, found creative solutions, and discovered treasures along the way. As I've traveled around the country speaking to women on marriage and sharing our creative solutions, many have told me they wished there was a book to help men understand their needs better. So, I started asking them to write down what they felt every husband should know. The women of America have spoken, or nearly one thousand of them have, and here are their answers:

EIGHT THINGS EVERY HUSBAND NEEDS TO KNOW

1. *Your wife needs you to be the spiritual leader of your home.*
2. *Your wife needs you to be her teammate in raising the kids and taking care of the home.*
3. *Your wife needs you to treat her like a princess.*
4. *Your wife needs you to communicate with her.*
5. *Your wife needs her friends and needs you to allow her time with the girls, but ultimately she wants you to be her best friend.*
6. *Your wife needs you to be a "triple A" encourager by giving her appreciation, affirmation, and admiration.*
7. *Your wife needs to feel emotionally filled before she desires to be sexually involved.*
8. *Your wife needs you to understand that there are some things you will never understand. This doesn't make either of you right or wrong—just different.*

When Art and I first got married, we viewed marriage as an overflowing treasure chest full of things like fun, security, companionship, adventure, good communication, and great sex. We were shocked to discover that our chest was empty. We now know that if our marriage is going to be full of great things, it is up to us to fill our marriage chest with great treasures. Having a great marriage takes time, creativity, and a willingness to understand the needs of the other person. That's where this book is going to help you. You can't possibly meet the needs of your wife and fill up your marriage treasure chest if you don't know what her needs and desires are.

Now that I've given you a list of things you need to know, let me inject two disclaimers. The first is that it is not enough for you to just read this book; you must apply this information. Make loving your wife a part of your everyday schedule just like brushing your teeth. You can't just brush your teeth once and expect to have fresh breath the rest of your life. The same is true with loving your wife.

The second disclaimer is that not all women are created alike. While most of these ideas will work great, your wife will have unique ways she needs to be loved. You need to discover these. The beauty of this book is that it will get you headed in the right direction and open up the lines of communication necessary to make these great discoveries.

Now, if you are like my husband, you are busy. So for the sake of time, I give you permission to put this book down for today. But, don't forget to do this home improvement project. At the end of each chapter you'll find these practical assignments that will help you go the extra mile as a husband.

HOME IMPROVEMENT—*1. Get a stick-it note and write the word "Perfect!" on it. Now, go stick it on top of the part of your wife's scale where the numbers are. This will score BIG points, but don't do it expecting anything in return.*

 THOUGHT FOR THE DAY—*One simple dandelion on a no-name day is worth more to me than a dozen roses on a Hallmark holiday.*—DONNA [JOLIET]

*Your wife
needs you to
be the spiritual
leader of
your home.*

CHAPTER 1

BECOMING A SPIRITUAL LEADER

G od designed marriage as a beautiful picture of Christ's relationship with His bride, the church. Just as Jesus is the spiritual leader of His bride, so should you be with your wife. In the surveys I collected from women, desiring the husband to be the spiritual leader of the home was one of the most common responses. When a man leads his home under God's direction, He becomes like Jesus to his family. He's not a larger-than-life dictator but rather a gentle, loving, wise leader. When a husband becomes a leader who models Jesus' character, a woman's heart feels safe enough to submit to that leadership. In this God-designed picture the husband and wife mutually complete one another, giving a beautiful picture of the oneness God intended for marriage.

Learning to love one another and meet each other's needs is important, because it strengthens a couple's relationship and allows them to remain true to their commitment. More important than strengthening the relationship with one another is keeping the covenant they made before God. As the husband and wife grow closer to God as individuals, God will more closely knit their hearts together. They will learn to love unconditionally and serve sacrificially as Jesus modeled in giving His life for His bride.

Never have I seen a more beautiful picture of this than in

a letter I read written by Dr. Robert McQuilken. This letter served as his resignation from his position of president of Columbia Bible College. He wrote:

My dear wife, Muriel, has been in failing mental health for about eight years. So far I have been able to carry both her ever-growing needs and my leadership responsibilities at CBC. But recently it has become apparent that Muriel is contented most of the time she is with me and almost none of the time I am away from her. It is not just "discontent." She is filled with fear—even terror—that she has lost me and goes in search for me when I leave home. So it is clear to me that she needs me now, full time.

Perhaps it would help you to understand if I shared with you what I shared at the time of my resignation in chapel. The decision was made, in a way, forty-two years ago when I promised to care for Muriel "in sickness and health . . . till death do us part." So, as I told the students and faculty, as a man of my word, integrity had something to do with it. But so does fairness. She has cared for me fully and sacrificially all these years; if I cared for her the next forty years I would not be out of debt. Duty, however, can be grim and stoic. But there is more; I love Muriel. She is a delight to me—her childlike dependence and confidence in me, her warm love, occasional flashes of wit I used to relish so, her happy spirit and tough resilience in the face of her continual distressing frustration. I do not have to care for her; I get to! It is a high honor to care for so wonderful a person.[1]

You may never have to care for the physical well-being of your wife as Dr. McQuilken described, but your wife needs to know that if you had to, you would do it with the same joy and integrity described above. More than caring for her physically, your wife needs to see you caring for your family's spiritual needs, as well. When a woman sees her husband daily submitting to God, reading his Bible, praying, and walking in a close personal relationship with Jesus, it is much easier for her to give him the respect he needs.

What I love about Dr. McQuilken's letter is it's written by a man who walks closely with Jesus and seeks to model his Master's character. When Muriel reached out for her husband's hand in times of terror and confusion, he became Jesus to her. His hands were tender, his words compassionate, his eyes full of love, and his heart full of joy. When your wife reaches out to take your hand, what does she feel in your touch? What does she hear from your lips? What does she see in your eyes? What does she know is in your heart? How can you be Jesus to her?

The amazing thing about being your wife's spiritual leader is not what you get from this position but what you have the privilege to give. Your wife needs your prayers, your wise counsel, your strength, and your courage. Penny from Decatur explained in her survey response: "Every husband needs to know that he is his family's spiritual umbrella, and that his wife and children are safest when they are underneath it."

Her comment reflects a biblical concept. Psalm 1:1–3 says, "Blessed is the man who does not walk in the counsel of the wicked or stand in the way of sinners or sit in the seat of mockers. But his delight is in the law of the LORD, and on his law he meditates day and night. He is like a tree planted by streams of water, which yields its fruit in season and whose leaf does not wither. Whatever he does prospers." Imagine your role as spiritual leader like that tree. You provide shelter during the storms of life. You are firmly planted so your wife can lean on you when she gets weary. You yield the fruits of the Spirit because you draw your nourishment from God's Word. You are steadfast and your leaves do not wither. Best of all you stand tall for God, and when your wife looks at you, it makes her desire to walk even closer in her own relationship with Jesus.

My husband, Art, has become a wonderful spiritual leader for our home. He faithfully prays for us, spends time with God, and has a contagious joyful spirit. One of the best things he does every night on his way home from work is to make a mental stop at his treasure tree. It's not a real tree but rather a point along the way home where he hangs all the troubles from his day. After dropping off his frustrations, setbacks, and stresses, he takes time to receive an extra dose of the fruits of the Spirit. Soon he's overflowing with these treasures and ready for home. Love, joy, peace, patience, kindness, goodness, faithfulness, gentleness, and self-control are, after all, what every wife longs for in her spiritual leader.

HOME IMPROVEMENT—*1. On your way home from work tonight, find a treasure tree spot where you can exchange the frustrations from your day for an extra dose of love, joy, peace, patience, kindness, goodness, faithfulness, and self-control. 2. Make visiting this tree part of your daily routine.*

 THOUGHT FOR THE DAY—*The most important thing a husband can do for his wife is to seek the Lord with his whole heart and being. If he puts God first, God will give him the strength and desire to be an awesome husband.*
—AMY [DUNLOP]

CHAPTER 2

PRAYING FOR YOUR WIFE

I still remember thinking his hands were magnificent, despite the fact that age had wrinkled and weakened them. I thought about all the amazing things these hands had done. They'd worked the farm and tended the fields. They'd faithfully provided for his wife and six children. They'd been brave and steadfast as he fought in wars protecting our country's freedom. They'd tenderly loved his wife and proudly welcomed each of his children into the world. These same hands wiped tears from his eyes as he watched his beloved wife pass on. Yes, I remember these hands well.

They belonged to my grandfather, with whom I had the privilege of living when I was in junior high. It was a rough time in my family. My father and mother were divorcing. Emotions were high and finances low. I thought the divorce was my fault and carried a burden of guilt and remorse. I'd been abused by another grandfather figure and had a hard time trusting anyone. I felt alone and vulnerable. But I always knew Grandpa was there for me. Quirky as his old age made him at times, he was there. More times than not you'd see him in his favorite chair by his bed pouring over the pages of his well-worn Bible.

Sometimes in the afternoon when I'd get home from

school, I'd feel especially low so I'd go see Grandpa. Though I was too big to fit comfortably on his lap, he'd use his aged hands to welcome me and hold me. Conversations were strained because his hearing was failing but his hands said everything I needed to hear, *I love you and you are welcome here with me.*

The most amazing thing I ever saw those wonderful hands do was to fold together in prayer. Grandpa was a praying man. He loved Jesus like few I've ever known, and he prayed for extended periods of time. In humble submission he'd fold his hands, bow his head, and lift his heart cries to a Savior he knew well.

Many years after Grandpa passed away, I was going through other struggles. I was angry about all the turmoil I'd had to endure as a child and jealous of my friends who'd grown up with more normal childhoods. I'd hear Christian friends talking about dads who'd prayed for them their whole lives and wondered if my dad had even prayed for me once. Chances are he had not. Then God gave me a precious memory that had gotten lost over the years . . . He reminded me of Grandpa's hands.

I wonder if your wife has ever had someone praying over her like my grandpa did for me. Let your hands leave a lasting legacy. More than just working hard and fighting daily battles, let them fold together in prayer.

A PRAYER FOR YOUR WIFE:

Loving Father,

Thank You for my wife and the unique person she is. Thank You for putting her into my life. Lord, I love her and accept her as she is just now, and release her to become the person You have designed in Your perfect will.

You have a plan and a calling upon her life; may she fulfill it to bring You glory.

I agree with the promises in Your Word. By the spiritual authority You have given to us as believers, I pray Your wonderful blessing for my wife.

You have set marriage to be a picture of Christ and His beloved. I want to model that kind of sacrifice, love, and dedication to You. May she find purpose and satisfaction in the shelter of our marriage.

Bless my wife anew with the reality of how much You love her. Give her a greater awareness of Your presence. You alone can meet her deepest needs.

Help me stand by her, both of us growing in love and faithfulness. When I believe she needs my direction or correction, let us both be honest in communication and open to Your wisdom and help.

Bless her with an increase of good health and energy. Bind

excessive tiredness and illness off of her. Bind confusion and discouragement off of her. Release her to the joy, peace, and contentment of Jesus. Release Your Holy Spirit's power into her life. Guide her to take a strong stand against the devil's deceptions; teach her to overcome by Your Word.

Each day we live shows us how much we need You. The world demands impossible things of us. Your Word gives us impossible things to do in our own strength. We are totally dependent on You and truly grateful to You. You do not ask us to do anything without making it possible. Yes, Father, how good You are!

We trust You for everything.

You will never leave us or forsake us, and You will take us to live with You forever. We are eternally grateful. Amen.[1]

Finally, there is no more powerful way to pray for your sweetheart than using scriptural prayers. Below I've listed some possibilities. The most important thing is that you commit to praying for her. If you aren't praying for her daily, who is?
Here are some suggested scriptural prayers:

■ That Christ may dwell in her heart through faith and that her life would be rooted and grounded in Christ's love (Ephesians 3:17).

■ That she would love you, her husband, as you need to be loved (Ephesians 5:33).

■ That she would rely on Christ to do exceedingly abundantly beyond all she asks or thinks, according to Christ's power in her (Ephesians 3:20).

■ That the Lord would establish the work of her hands (Psalm 90:17).

■ That she would not grow weary in doing good, for in due season she will reap a reward if she does not lose heart (Galatians 6:9).

■ That she would walk not in the flesh but according to the Spirit. That the fruits of the Spirit would become more and more evident in her life (Galatians 5:22–23).

■ That she would take on the full armor of God and be able to stand firm against the schemes of Satan (Ephesians 6:10–18).

■ That she would not be deceived by the lusts and sins of the world. That she would put aside all filthiness and all wickedness and in humility receive the Word of God. Then may she be a doer of the Word and not a hearer only (James 1:14–16, 21–23).

■ That she would be a good mother who correctly disciplines, wisely trains, and gently loves her children (Proverbs 3:12; Proverbs 23:24; Proverbs 29:17).

■ That she would call on the name of the Lord to be her deliverer, her strength, the One in whom she trusts, her shield, and her salvation (Psalm 18:2–3).

■ That God would perfect, confirm, strengthen, and establish her to be the woman He created her to be (1 Peter 5:10).

HOME IMPROVEMENT—*Ask your wife how you can pray specifically for her today. Hold her hand and pray aloud for her. Let her know that your hands will fold in prayer for her often.*

 THOUGHT FOR THE DAY—*The prayer of a righteous man is powerful and effective.*—*[JAMES 5:16]*

CHAPTER 3

YOUR WIFE IS NOT THE ENEMY

I t was a perfect vacation. The mountains were breathtaking. The ski conditions perfect. The food was fabulous and the evenings by the fire romantic. We acted like two sweethearts, holding hands, laughing at private jokes, and stealing kisses on the ski lift. *I'll love this man forever,* I thought as I thanked God for giving me such an amazing husband.

Scene change.

It started out as a great vacation. A house on the beach with our closest friends. Our kids were having a blast. We'd brought sitters along and were excited about adults' nights out at nice restaurants. The weather was perfect and before long we were all sporting golden tans. Then a misunderstanding between Art and me ended in hurt feelings and cold silence. Summer romance was down the tube, and Art was down the hall sleeping away from me. *Why is he so insensitive and mean?* I cried myself to sleep asking God what I did to deserve this kind of marriage.

Will the real TerKeurst marriage please come forward?

I'll love him forever or *Why is he so insensitive and mean . . .* Which story best exemplifies our marriage? Both. We've experienced times of oneness where we seem to understand what makes one another tick and other times of isolation where all we seem to do is tick one another off.

The most important lesson we've learned in our years of

marriage is that we are not each other's enemies. At times we've hurt one another deeply, because I saw him as my enemy and he saw me as his, but we were deceived. Understanding this deception and discovering the real enemy has helped transform our marriage.

Ephesians 6:10–12 says, "Finally, be strong in the Lord and in his mighty power. Put on the full armor of God so that you can take your stand against the devil's schemes. For our struggle is not against flesh and blood, but against the rulers, against the authorities, against the powers of this dark world and against the spiritual forces of evil in the heavenly realms." Satan's attacks cause the troubles we face in our relationships, not each other. But if we are willing to plug into God's power source, we will be able to stand against Satan's attacks.

It is vital to be "strong in the Lord and in his mighty power." To experience His "mighty power" (that makes Satan tuck tail and run), we must allow God to control our lives. We must take time to read our Bible and get serious about praying and listening to God. I heard a quote once that helped tie these principles together, "Reading the Bible gives you the vocabulary to understand what the Holy Spirit wants to tell you."[1] John 14:26 affirms this: "The Holy Spirit . . . will teach you all things and will remind you of everything I have said to you."

What does this mean for our marriages? We don't have to have all the answers; we just have to stay in touch with the One who does. He will teach, guide, and convict us. He'll help us forgive and show us how to love.

Second, we must put on the full armor of God. This is something that should get your warrior blood pumping. God made your heart for adventure and battle so let's make sure we dress to kill.

WE ARE TO PUT ON THE BELT OF TRUTH

The truth is that you and your wife are beloved children of the Most High King. The truth is that what causes conflict in your marriage is that Satan hates anything God loves. He is scheming with your weaknesses in mind to cause division in your marriage. The truth is though *we* are weak, *God* is strong. The truth is that God loves you, God loves her, and He desires for you to love one another.

THE BREASTPLATE OF RIGHTEOUSNESS PROTECTS OUR HEARTS

To be righteous means to act in a morally correct way. We need to keep our hearts pure and obedient. What's the best way to check our heart's condition? Listen to what is coming out of our mouths. Luke 6:45 says, "The good man brings good out of the good stored up in his heart, and the evil man brings evil things out of the evil stored up in his heart. For out of the overflow of his heart his mouth speaks." Listen to what you are saying to your loved ones. Are the words encouraging, edifying, and loving? If not, seek to repair this chink in your armor.

OUR FEET ARE FITTED WITH THE READINESS THAT COMES FROM THE GOSPEL OF PEACE

This is all about our pursuit to press on and tell others about Christ. One of the best ways to tell others about the gospel and its life changing truths is to live a life that reveals Christ's love. In a day when a happy and fulfilling marriage is so rare, what a powerful witness your healthy marriage could be.

WE ARE TO TAKE UP OUR SHIELD OF FAITH

This is the shield with which you can extinguish all the flaming arrows of the evil one. Insults, frustrations, aggravations. The shield of faith reduces these attacks of the evil one by reminding us to look beyond here-and-now difficulties. It's the daily irritations that drag down our marriages. She makes the toilet paper roll from the bottom rather than the top. She washed a red shirt with my white underwear. She steals the covers at night. Having faith means keeping an eternal perspective, laughing at our shortcomings, and choosing to love despite differences.

THEN WE HAVE THE HELMET OF SALVATION— PROTECTION FOR OUR MINDS

Satan loves to make us doubt: doubt God, doubt our salvation, doubt our commitment to our spouse. How easily people have been deceived into thinking they've married the wrong person just because they experience rocky times. Since marriage is a physical representation of Christ and the church, Satan wants us to doubt our union. To destroy a marriage and the love between man and wife is to distort what God intended as a picture of His love for us. To protect your mind from damaging thoughts about your marriage and to keep your thought life pure, meditate on Scriptures. (See Deuteronomy 6:6.)

FINALLY, WE HAVE THE SWORD OF THE SPIRIT

We must have a commanding knowledge of Scripture. Start today memorizing Scriptures that you find helpful when you are tempted or when you get angry with your wife. Become so familiar with these words of God that you are able to recall and use them instantly to refute the lies of the enemy. Don't get bogged down into thinking I'm telling you to memorize the whole Bible; just start simply and realistically.

Remember, the precious beautiful woman you curl up next to tonight is not your enemy. She's not the one causing your frustrations and heartaches. She's the beauty who longs to be rescued. She's getting as hurt in this spiritual battle as you are. At times she's afraid and feels alone. She needs a man who will not fight her but fight the fire-breathing beast who seeks to destroy you both. She needs a knight in shining armor.

HOME IMPROVEMENT—*In bed tonight hold your wife until she falls asleep. Then spend some time looking at your breathtaking princess. Pray that God would teach you how to be a brave knight and mentally dress yourself for the spiritual battle. Commit to fighting* for, *not* against, *your Beauty.*

 THOUGHT FOR THE DAY—*Every husband needs to know that he is his family's spiritual umbrella and that his wife and children are safest when they are underneath it.*

—*PENNY [DECATUR]*

Your wife needs

you to be her

teammate in

raising the kids

and taking care

of the home.

CHAPTER 4

CALLING ALL RECRUITS

I f your wife is a stay-at-home mom, there are some things you should never say and some questions you should never ask. One such question might pop out of your mouth when you trip over toys strewn across the floor, "What have you done all day?" How this question will hurt your wife. To you, it is natural to wonder how the house could look this way if she's been home all day. To her, you are saying she is a lousy wife, mother, and housekeeper, and maybe that you wish you'd married Brenda Sue down the street.

This question can cause devastation to an already weary and spent mommy. My favorite response to my husband is, "I'm doing the best I can." For most women this is true. We are doing the best we can with all the demands placed on us. I do desire for our home to be a haven for my husband, but some days it doesn't work out that way. What I need from him when he gets home, especially on disaster days, is a big hug, a big thank-you, and a big helping hand.

If your wife works, she is going to need help. With only twenty-four hours in any given day and a to-do list that stretches a mile long, no wonder she's tired all the time. Could you take some of her to-dos for her?

"Now wait just one minute!" you say. "According to the Bible, isn't my role to be the provider and hers to be the keeper of the home?" First Timothy 5:8 says, "If anyone does not provide for his relatives, and especially for his immediate family, he has denied the faith and is worse than an unbeliever." Titus 2:4–5 instructs "women to love their husbands and children, to be self-controlled and pure, to be busy at home, to be kind, and to be subject to their husbands."

The Bible points to clear and distinct roles that are to be filled by the man and the woman. But the Bible goes on in Titus 2:6–7 to instruct men, "Similarly, encourage the young men to be self-controlled. In everything set them an example by doing what is good." If you expect your wife to serve in the areas of the home and kids, then you should "set the example" and be willing to help. First Peter 3:7 says, "Husbands, in the same way be considerate as you live with your wives." Considerate. That's what a wife needs: for her husband to consider all she is responsible for and all that she does and to find ways to help her.

I love a story that came across my e-mail recently. Before you read it, though, I must tell you I don't like the word *chauvinist* and would not use it unless it was part of the story's original text. However, I think the story makes a good point.

Mary was married to a male chauvinist. They both worked full time, but he never did anything around the house and certainly not any housework. *That,* he declared, was woman's work.

But one evening Mary arrived home from work to find the children bathed, a load of wash in the washing machine and another in the dryer, dinner on the stove and a beautifully set table, complete with flowers.

She was astonished, and she immediately wanted to

know what was going on. It turned out that Charley, her husband, had read a magazine article that suggested working wives would be more romantically inclined if they weren't so tired from having to do all the housework in addition to holding down a full-time job.

The next day, she couldn't wait to tell her friends in the office. "How did it work out?" they asked.

"Well, it was a great dinner," Mary said. "Charley even cleaned up, helped the kids with their homework, folded the laundry and put everything away."

"But what about afterward?" her friends wanted to know.

"It didn't work out," Mary said. "Charley was too tired."[1]

I bet Charley was tired, and I bet your wife is too. Just for fun, let's write out a few of the things your wife may do in a day.

CHILDREN: Wake them up, get them dressed, feed them, hug them, pack snacks and lunches, transport them to and from (and back to and back from), bathe them or remind them to bathe, plan their birthday party, make their doctor's and dentist's appointments, kiss their wounds, help mend a teen's broken heart, listen for opportunities to share about Jesus' love, tell them what a great dad they have, help with homework, monitor their TV watching and time on the computer, feed them again, say nighttime prayers, tuck them into bed, kiss them good night.

FOOD: Check current stock, make a list of needed items, clip coupons, go to the store, compare prices, peel screaming two-year-old off the floor after she tells him he may not have a five-pound bag of chocolate chips, decide which side items go best with main dishes she's preparing, debate whether or not to get that ice cream she's been craving, stand in a slow-moving line, purchase the groceries, transport them home, make five or six trips to the car to get them into the house, put everything away, pull half of it back out to make dinner, mess the kitchen she spent half the morning cleaning, call everyone to dinner, set the table, call everyone to dinner again, serve the food, clear the table, store leftovers, and clean everything again.

These are just two of the many categories on your wife's daily to-do list. We didn't even get to cleaning, organizing, paperwork, and miscellaneous extras not to mention finding time for prayer and Bible study.

I'm not trying to guilt you into becoming more domestic. I'm not wanting to overload your already overflowing to-do list. I'm just reminding you to be aware of the demands placed on your wife, to be willing to help cheerfully when you can, and as the Bible commands, simply to be considerate.

HOME IMPROVEMENT—*After all this talk of to-dos the last thing you want is another assignment, so for today just thank your wife for all she does.*

 THOUGHT FOR THE DAY—*No matter how many times you tell me I'm important, or that you think of me through the day, or that our family is a priority to you . . . it's meaningless unless your actions match your words.*—DANA [SIDNEY]

CHAPTER 5

TOUCH HER HEART BY
SPENDING TIME WITH THE KIDS

W e found out we were having our second baby when our first was a few months old, and I was in shock. The doctor said, "Congratulations, you're going to have a baby." All I could think was, *I already have a baby and I'm overwhelmed with just her. How will I manage two?* Art was thrilled and assured me that everything would work out fine.

Soon Ashley was born. She was beautiful and all my worries melted when I saw her. Though it was challenging managing two small children, the Lord, my friends, and family helped carry me through the rough days. Art was a tremendous help. We were now a family of four and feeling blessed.

Then when Ashley was six weeks old, she became ill. The doctor admitted us to the hospital where during the next week she got worse and worse. Finally, we were taken to the Intensive Care Unit where the doctor told us there was a good chance we'd lose her. Ashley's immune system had gotten confused and in an attempt to fight off an allergic reaction, started fighting off good things as well. Before one of her emergency surgeries, the doctors gave us a few minutes to be alone with Ashley . . . to tell her good-bye. They told us it was unlikely she would make it through.

I remember standing over her crib with tears pouring from

my eyes telling God, *No. You cannot take her!* I was hurt and desperate. He could save her. My soul cried out, *God, please save her!* Art held me as we prayed over her together, and then they took her away.

Art helped me outside for fresh air. Out in the parking lot, he gently cupped my face in his hands and asked, "Lysa, whose child is she?"

"She's our child," I replied weakly.

To which he quietly said, "No, Lysa, whose child is she?"

It took nearly all the strength I had to finally say, "She's God's child."

He looked into my eyes and said, "She was His to give and she is His to take. He's entrusted her to us for a little while, but ultimately we have to leave her in God's hands. If He leaves her here with us, we will be thankful. But if He chooses to take her, He is still faithful and still worthy of our trust."

Through my sobs I said, "OK. God, she's yours."

As a mother, that was the hardest and most profound lesson I've learned. As a father, I think when Art spoke those words something clicked deep within his soul, and he realized what an awesome thing it is to be a father. God did spare our Ashley, and today she is a healthy, active first-grader. We are thankful, but still we hold our children with open hands entrusting them to God every day.

We learned many things through that experience, but the one thing I want to focus on here is the fact that God has entrusted these precious little ones to us. As parents we have such awesome jobs to care for, nurture, teach, and help mold these little ones into people who love the Lord and others. Many responsibilities will naturally fall on your wife if she is the one who spends more time with them. But please don't shy away from being involved in your children's lives. Your wife needs your help and your children need your influence.

Little boys need to have their daddy tell them they have what it takes to be a man. It's difficult for a woman to give this type of blessing to her son. He needs his father to model what it means to be a godly man who loves the rough and tough things of life but at the same time can be tender and compassionate. Patrick Morley says, "Teachers, preachers, coaches, and peers form the supporting cast, but the single greatest influence on the manhood of a boy is his dad."[1]

Little girls need to hear their father tell them they are beautiful and worthy to be someone's princess. While a mommy blesses her daughter through teaching feminine things, only a daddy can bless a daughter's heart with masculine affirmation. I can assure you if she does not hear this blessing from her daddy, she'll look for it when she's older from other men.

"Good parenting provides no guarantee our children will turn out right, but bad parenting often means they will turn out wrong."[2] You have the opportunity to pass on a godly legacy to your children—whether or not one was passed to you. If you had incredible parents, thank the Lord and honor them by passing your heritage to your children. If your parents weren't the example they could have been, forgive them and break the cycle by becoming the parent you longed for.

Don't look at the times when you watch the kids as mere baby-sitting. When you have time alone with the kids, realize it is an investment with incredible returns. Plus, time away for your wife is an investment in your marriage. When she gets away, it recharges her batteries; she'll be a better wife and mom when she returns.

Your wife knows she can do a lot for her children, but she needs you to be her teammate and give them what only you can give. It will touch her heart in ways you can't imagine to see you invest yourself in your little ones' lives.

Deuteronomy 6:6–7 says, "These commandments that I give you today are to be upon your hearts. Impress them on your children. Talk about them when you sit at home and when you walk along the road, when you lie down and when you get up." In other words, God is asking you to be a godly influence on your children when you're with them at home and when you take them out in public. Model good character and solid values when you tuck them into bed and when you wake them each morning. There is no other way to be this kind of "impression" on your children than spending time with them.

HOME IMPROVEMENT—*Write a personal note of blessing to each of your children in your own handwriting. Frame your note and put it in their room.*

THOUGHT FOR THE DAY—*I am so attracted to my husband when he spends time and shows affection to my children. I love watching him be a dad, enjoying the little persons God created out of our love. I love to watch him take our twelve-year-old daughter out on a lunch date. I love to watch him share a silly joke with my seven-year-old and wrestle with our three-year-old. I try to lock that picture frame of time in my mind and heart.*—PAM [BURLINGTON]

43

CHAPTER 6

EVERY HOME NEEDS A PROVIDER

W hen we moved into our home it was an easy move. A bed, two dressers, some rent-to-own den furniture left from my husband's college days, a dog cage, and the oldest microwave you've ever seen were among our few possessions. Our old microwave just didn't fit into our new home, with its new appliances. So, I requested a new one. Art explained a new microwave was not in the budget. Since the old one still worked, a new one could wait. I pouted but agreed.

When Art said the old one still worked, that was true in that it had the capacity to heat up food, but neither the timer nor any of the buttons worked. The old thing had been in the family for years and for some reason Art felt attached. Day after day, meal after meal, we continued to place our food in the ancient cookery and count off the seconds in our head.

Then one day we had a sitter, and I forgot to tell her about the timer not working. She placed a biscuit in the microwave and by the time she remembered it, the biscuit had been reduced to a lump of charred remains. Black smoke filled the house. There is no smell quite like over-microwaved food. Every time we tried to use the microwave after that, the smell again filled the house.

Finally, I thought, *now we'll surely be able to justify a new microwave.* I researched the model I wanted and presented Art with what I thought was an airtight case.

"Nope, a new microwave is still not in the budget." As he said this, Art picked up the old, smelly microwave and proceeded out to the garage. He set it on a plastic kid's table off to the side and plugged it in. "See, good as new," he said with a big smile. "It still works well enough to heat up our food and the smell won't bother anyone out here in the garage."

I was stunned. Did he expect me to walk out to the garage, place my food into this awful thing, hold my breath as I ran inside to escape the smell, stand by the back door to count off the approximate heating time, hold my breath again, dash through the now fume-filled garage, press the stop button, and then come in to enjoy my meal? Are you kidding? I was about to give him a real earful when something stopped me dead in my tracks.

Suddenly I remembered, many years before, my mom sitting at our kitchen table surrounded by bills, crying. Since she and Dad separated, Mom was a single mom holding down several jobs. Even so, there was not enough to make ends meet. Accounts were overdrawn and bills were late. Though I was small, I knew we were in trouble.

That was a horrible feeling—one I'd never had since being married to Art. He had never let bills go unpaid. He had not gotten us in over our head. He managed our money by setting a budget and sticking to it. So what if we couldn't get a new microwave. My reaction suddenly took an about-face as I smiled and said, "Good idea."

For another year we went without a new microwave. It became a source of entertainment when we had guests over.

When the old thing finally gave out, I think we were sad to see it go. The new white microwave we saved for and finally purchased doesn't have nearly as much character as the old one (but it does have a really cool popcorn button).

As you help your wife around the house and with the kids, don't ignore the importance of being a good financial steward of the resources God has entrusted to you. Your wife needs you to provide financial security. Her heart will feel safe to know you will provide for her and the children. Your children need to witness God's plan for handling finances. They need to see you give to God first, save for the future, and manage your spending. Not only do they need to see you do it, they need you to take time teaching them how to handle money properly.

Set a realistic budget with your wife's input. Make it a team effort. Ask her what things she would like to save toward and be sure to include those in your plan. Maybe she'd like to save for a new bedroom set, new curtains, a special vacation—or even a new microwave.

Being your family's provider means more than bringing home a paycheck. It means finding God's balance for your life so you can properly invest both your time and your money. Remember the wisdom in Matthew 6:33 that says, "Seek first his kingdom and his righteousness, and all these things will be given to you as well."

HOME IMPROVEMENT—*If you struggle with finances, contact Crown Financial Ministries at: (888) 455-1552 to request information on family budgeting. Sit down with your wife and study the materials together. If you already live by a budget, review it with your wife. Ask her if she feels it is realistic. Ask her if there is anything she would like to be saving toward.*

 THOUGHT FOR THE DAY—*Wives would rather have more of you than more from you . . . time together is a priceless gift.*—ANGEE [VALDOSTA]

Your wife

needs you to

treat her like

a princess.

CHAPTER 7

WHO SAYS YOUR WIFE
IS A PRINCESS?

A brilliant, temperamental forty-one-year-old former monk and a strong-willed, sharp-tongued twenty five-year-old former nun. Not exactly what you'd call "match made in heaven."

When Martin Luther married Katharina Von Bora in 1525, their friends and family were shocked. Katharina was the last of twelve nuns escaping from their convent whom Luther was helping find jobs or husbands. Luther kept trying to find her a husband, but his choices didn't suit Katie. She told him that she could see only two possible options: Amsdorf, one of Luther's friends, or Luther himself.

By this time Luther's marital status was becoming somewhat of a problem for him. His enemies were circulating rumors about his "harem," suggesting impropriety in his care for the runaway nuns. Luther's friends thought he was leaving himself open to unnecessary criticism and speculation when he didn't practice what he preached. (Luther advocated marriage as a biblical institution and declared there was no prohibition of marriage for those in God's service.) Even his elderly parents, desperate for grandchildren, were pressuring him. It didn't look hopeful: Luther was stubborn, and he had been a bachelor all his life.

He shocked them all when he decided to take the plunge. Within three days of having the idea, Martin and Katharina were married. It wasn't a romantic affair, more of a marriage of convenience for both of them. As Luther noted it would "please his father, rile the pope, make angels laugh, devils weep, and would seal his testimony." Even so, he warned his bride-to-be that he might be burned at the stake, and she with him. Katie was undeterred.

Although their marriage came about out of necessity, it quickly became a full-blown romance. Luther referred lovingly to Katie and their children in his writings. Visitors noted the humor and warmth in the couple's witty exchanges.

As a single man, Luther had written of marriage as being necessary to satisfy the needs of the flesh. But as a married man, he spoke of the spiritual blessings and challenges marriage brings. He grew concerned about husbands he observed who showed no love or care for their wives.

"Of course the Christian should love his wife!" Luther exclaimed. "He is supposed to love his neighbor, and since his wife is his nearest neighbor, she should be his deepest love. She should also be his dearest friend."[1]

For such a rocky start, Martin and Katie Luther did have a great marriage. And what great insight Luther had in elevating this unwanted nun into his beloved wife. Though I'm sure it was quite a process, Luther learned to love her as Christ commands, and in the process he fell more deeply in love than he could have imagined. I can just imagine what that did for Katie's self-esteem and sense of worth. Once she was an unwanted runaway nun, but then she became someone's beloved princess.

When Dr. James Dobson, founder of Focus on the Family, was asked by author Joyce Landorf, "What would you change about women in general if you could wave some sort of magic wand?" He replied:

> If I could write a prescription for the women of the world, I would provide each one of them with a healthy dose of self-esteem and personal worth (taken three times a day until the symptoms disappear). I have no doubt that this is their greatest need. . . . If women felt genuinely respected in their role as wives and mothers, they would not need to abandon it for something better. If they felt *equal* with men in personal worth, they would not need to be equivalent to men in responsibility. If they could only bask in the dignity and status granted them by their Creator, then their femininity would be valued as their greatest asset, rather than scorned as an old garment to be discarded. Without question, the future of a nation depends on how it sees its women, and I hope we teach our little girls to be glad they were chosen by God for the special pleasures of womanhood.[2]

Later in a counseling session with a woman who was struggling with low self-esteem, Dr. Dobson asked if she'd ever shared her feelings with her husband. Through her tears she replied, "I have been married for eight years, but my husband has no idea I feel so inadequate!" When he wrote about this woman in *What Wives Wish Their Husbands Knew About Women*, Dr. Dobson said, "Inferiority is the best kept secret of the year, yet it is one which wives wish their husbands comprehended."[3]

Katie Luther could have carried that burdensome "unwanted" feeling with her all her life, but she didn't. She thrived in her role as Martin Luther's wife. She thrived in his obvious love for her. Maybe that was the secret of their wonderful marriage. He made his love so obvious. He esteemed Katie in the way he treated her and in the way he respected her in private and public. He made the decision to be the husband of a happy wife; thus, he was.

Granted your wife's relationship with the Lord must be her soul's source of worth, but you can do wonders for her in making your love obvious to her. You can become the husband of a happier wife simply by deciding in your heart who she is. Ask yourself, who is that funny creature who's invaded your manhood with ponytail scrunchies, perfume bottles, glue guns, nail polish, and decorating magazines? Who is this that sends you on the most embarrassing of errands down the feminine hygiene aisle at the grocery store? Who is it that spends hours in front of the bathroom mirror debating one of the great questions of life: to perm or not to perm (translation: should she keep her hair straight or get a "perm" to make it curly)?

She is a daughter of the Most High King. She is a Princess, created in the image of God—a royal heir of the eternal throne. God made her beautiful and uniquely gifted. She was made with you in mind, with a heart that yearns for your adoration and acceptance. She's been entrusted to your care to love, honor, and cherish "until death do you part."

HOME IMPROVEMENT—*Ask your wife for a picture of herself as a little girl. Tuck it into your wallet and look at it often.*

 THOUGHT FOR THE DAY—*I heard once, "Treat your wife like a queen and you'll be the king of your house."* —*DIANE [ST. PETERS]*

CHAPTER 8

WHAT ALL PRINCESSES
EAT FOR BREAKFAST

C heerios. It was a simple enough request. Tonya was grateful Jim offered to run to the store for a few things, so she carefully listed each item she needed and thanked him for helping her. Upon his return, Tonya was a bit concerned by the deviations from her list. Jim was excited about the good deals he'd found by buying things in bulk and getting generic brands instead of name brands. Tonya didn't say anything until she pulled out the box of generic Cheerios. Now, she could no longer hold back her tongue. Tears filled her eyes as these thoughts ran through her mind: *Cheerios, real Cheerios is my favorite breakfast. He knows this. What was he thinking? He doesn't think I'm worth real Cheerios. I'm not worth the extra dollar it would have cost. I'm not even worth a dollar.* Suddenly she blurted out, "You don't value me at all!"

What was Jim thinking? He was excited to get the most bang for his buck. Simple mistake with no emotional implications intended. Why did this hurt Tonya? Because Tonya wanted Jim to treasure her and treat her like a princess. She wanted him to think of ways to make her feel special. It's not so much that he lavish her with expensive things. But she needed to know Jim thought she was worth anything her heart desired even though they might never be able to afford those things. When he could afford something, he should make the investment. He could have afforded the one extra dollar it would have cost to buy her favorite cereal. His princess likes Cheerios. What does your princess like?

All women desire to be valued. Your wife is constantly reading the unspoken cues you give off as to whether or not you cherish her, treasure her, and value her. The total of these cues equals whether or not she feels loved. If she senses you value her as a person, not for what she does but for who she is, she'll feel affirmed and fulfilled in her role as your wife. If she feels taken for granted, ignored, and devalued, she'll start to build walls to shut you out and protect herself from getting hurt. The danger is that other people may be telling her the things she longs to hear from you. Every time someone else tells her she's beautiful, smart, talented, witty, etc., she mentally weighs the comments of others against your cues. Make sure the heart of your princess is drawn only to you.

Bill McCartney, founder of Promise Keepers, said there was one statement he heard from a pulpit that changed the course of his life: "If you want to measure the worth of a man's effectiveness in life, all you have to do is look on the countenance of his wife." Bill looked at his wife, Lyndi, and was crushed by the sadness and pain he saw in her eyes. Bill said, "Hit hard by this sudden realization, I could only sit and weep. Soon thereafter I would resign my position as football coach of the University of Colorado, to finally learn, by the grace of God, what it meant to be a *real* man. I had been knocked off my lifelong course of selfish pursuits and sent sailing in an entirely different direction—to begin a new life of honoring and loving my faithful and precious wife."[1]

What do you see when you look on the countenance of your wife? For years my husband looked upon my discouraged and sad countenance. It wasn't until God got hold of both of our expectations that we learned what God intended in our marriage. He desires the two of us to mutually complete and serve one another. In doing this the two of us will come together and glorify God. There is no more beautiful picture than two becoming one and drawing others to Christ. Art has given me the gift of believing in my value as a daughter of the Most High King. I am able to be the woman God created me to be because of the love and support of my husband. I help complete him to become all God intended him to be.

So what do all princesses eat for breakfast? I have no idea. What I do know is this: Don't get overwhelmed with the big picture of figuring your wife out. Just walk day to day discovering what makes her smile and serve her as your princess. Realize it's the small things that count. Make it your mission to know what makes her feel valued and loved. If your wife likes real Cheerios, then by all means buy her real Cheerios.

HOME IMPROVEMENT—*Ask your wife to make a list of ten things you could do that would make her feel loved. After she completes this list, schedule these things in your calendar. Maybe you can do one per week for the next ten weeks.*

THOUGHT FOR THE DAY—*Tell your wife she is the most precious gift God has ever given you.*—TRUDY [CALIFORNIA]

CHAPTER 9

YOU ARE HER PRINCE CHARMING

Almost every woman can recall a time during her girl-hood when she dreamed of a prince who would ride into her life, sweep her off her feet, and carry her off into the sunset. It happened for Cinderella, Snow White, Belle, and the list goes on. Our minds are programmed from a young age that it will happen to us. Then one day you came, probably not on a horse, but nonetheless you came, her Prince Charming.

The only thing is, in the storybooks, the prince and his beloved ride off into the sunset while the words "and they lived happily ever after" dance across the page. We never hear how things go after that. The falling in love part is fun, but what about after the storybook wedding? Did they have to work through personality differences and financial struggles? Did either of them have morning breath? Did she gain a few unwanted pounds and did his thick hair ever thin? Did they have differing opinions about child rearing, church-going, or whether a cookie is better with chocolate chunks or chocolate chips?

Chances are they did, and our marriages do too. It is appropriate that we call the process of romance "falling in love." That gives us a clue that it's not going to be easy the whole way through. Think about the word *falling*—have you ever heard of someone falling into anything without a few bumps and bruises?

For some there are more bumps and bruises than others. Art and I have had more than our share. One thing we've learned is how important it is for each of us to rely on God's steadfast, never-changing love. While we love each other deeply, there always will be ways our love for each other falls short. You see, only God can be God. If our love for each other were altogether perfect and fulfilling, we wouldn't need God. Only God can give you what your deepest longings cry out for.

Some people search their whole lives for the perfect "soulmate," thinking if they found just the right match, all their needs would be met and they would finally be happy. In our throwaway society, many marriages are discarded when one or both partners realize their partner cannot meet their expectations. But no human relationship can fill the God-sized void we all have in our hearts.

Stan and his wife, Molly, were friends of ours for several of our early marriage years. They were active in church and even leaders in our Sunday school class where Stan led a men's accountability group and was respected for his extensive knowledge of the Bible. On the outside their marriage seemed picture-perfect. They had a thriving business, were devoted church members, had a growing family, and enjoyed what seemed to be a happy marriage.

But unbeknownst to his wife or any of us, tiny cracks were forming in Stan's foundation. While he had lots of God in his head, he had lots of questions in his heart. He grew restless and discontent. Soon he'd rationalized his way into the arms of another woman. Before long he left Molly, his children, and his church family for this seemingly perfect love that he'd found. We were all stunned, and Molly was left devastated and heartbroken.

What was Stan looking for? He was looking to have his deepest heart cries answered and fulfilled. For a time it seemed this new relationship was going to meet his needs, right all his wrongs, and bring excitement into his life. Maybe for a while its pleasures seemed promising. But then the excitement waned and the newness wore off, and Stan started seeking pleasure in yet another woman's arms.

I don't know what ever happened to Stan but I do know this: He will never find what he's looking for until he enters into a real relationship with the Lord. A relationship where his head knowledge of God is matched by his heart's surrender to Him. Only God can fill a man's deepest desires and prove to be unfailing in every way. Beth Moore says, "The Word of God uses the phrase unfailing love *thirty-two times,* and not once is it attributed to humans. Every single use of the phrase refers to God and God alone. As rich as is the love that others can extend, only God's love is unfailing."[1]

Do you ever catch yourself wondering if the grass might be greener in other pastures? Do you ever feel restless and discontented? Do you ever spend more time focusing on the negatives of your wife more than her positives? This is dangerous ground. Satan is waiting to trap you in these kinds of feelings. Colossians 3:1–4 says, "Since, then, you have been raised with Christ, set your hearts on things above, where

Christ is seated at the right hand of God. Set your minds on things above, not on earthly things. For you died, and your life is now hidden with Christ in God. When Christ, who is your life, appears, then you also will appear with him in glory."

Did you catch that? You are an heir of the King. You are a prince, not made in the likeness of a storybook fairytale character but made in the likeness of almighty God. You will appear with Christ "in glory." Therefore, set your mind and heart on thinking thoughts that honor Christ. Colossians 3:12–15 instructs us by saying, "Therefore, as God's chosen people, holy and dearly loved, clothe yourselves with compassion, kindness, humility, gentleness, and patience. Bear with each other and forgive whatever grievances you may have against one another. Forgive as the Lord forgave you. And over all these virtues put on love, which binds them all together in perfect unity. Let the peace of Christ rule in your hearts."

In my *NIV Life Application Study Bible,* the commentary on these verses says, "The word *rule* comes from the language of athletics: Paul tells us to let Christ's peace be the umpire or referee in our hearts. Our hearts are the center of conflict because there our feelings and desires clash—our fears and hopes, distrust and trust, jealousy and love. How can we live with these constant conflicts and live as God wants? Paul explains that we must decide between conflicting elements using the rule of peace—which choice will promote peace in our souls?"[2]

■ What choices are you in the process of making regarding your marriage?

■ Will you take your rightful place as a Prince of the King?

■ Will you choose the heart of your princess over all others?

■ Will you remain faithful in your pursuit of godliness?

If so, your marriage will be a beautiful example that happily-ever-afters really do exist.

HOME IMPROVEMENT—*Record your answers to the above questions here:*

_____

_____

_____

_____

_____

_____

_____

_____

_____

_____

_____

_____

_____

_____

_____

THOUGHT FOR THE DAY—*Make sure your words and actions make it clear to your children that you dearly love and respect their mother. This is what I sense from the teenagers that I teach. They are longing for a father to set an example of how to treat a woman.*—BRENDA [ROCKWELL]

Your wife

needs you to

communicate

with her.

CHAPTER 10

PLAYING THE CONVERSATION GAME

I love playing games. I've even been on "The Price Is Right." Okay, not very impressive, especially since after my name was called and I went screaming all the way down front, I stayed in contestants' row for the rest of the show. But everyone's got to have fifteen minutes of fame.

I didn't fair much better in the conversation game during the early years of my marriage. A typical conversation then might have gone like this:

Lysa: Hi, honey, how was your day?

Art: Good.

Lysa: Mine too. I took Hope and Ashley for their well checkups today. (Meaning I took the girls to the doctor not because they were sick but because it was time for their annual physicals.)

Art: (Silently wondering what our water well needed to be checked for and how our daughters fit into the same sentence.)

Lysa: (Feeling a little frustrated at his silence, which I

interpret as a lack of caring.) And, they were fine . . . (thinking: *Not that you seem to care.*)

Art: (Still silently wondering what our well water needed to be checked for and how our daughters fit into it.)

Lysa: Anyhow, (obviously annoyed), on my way to the doctor's office I was driving down Providence Road, and I noticed all the trees had black tape wrapped around them. It appears to be some sort of pest control treatment. Do you think our trees could be in danger of these bugs? Because if so, I think I'd like to try this tape stuff, which is probably a lot safer than spraying chemicals that could harm the children. You know I just don't think our government is doing enough to protect our kids from dangerous pesticides. So, do you think I should spend extra money at the grocery store for organic produce? If so, I'll need you to add some money to my grocery budget.

Art: (Wondering how the well, our daughters, the trees on Providence Road, and the government's stand on pesticides could end in a request to spend more money. He decides to play it safe.) I don't know, honey; I'll have to think about it.

Lysa: (Astonished at his lack of concern for our family's health begins to cry.) You'll have to think about what? We are talking about our daughters' lives here and all you can say is you'll think about it!

Art: (Baffled, still not understanding how any of this relates to our daughters' lives but clearly understanding I'm asking for more money again.) Why are you so emotional, and why are you always nagging me for more money? (He realizes he shouldn't have said nagging, remembering he got something thrown at him the last time he used that word. He regrets his choice of words and ducks just in case.)

Lysa: Nagging? You call caring for our children, *nagging?* You are so insensitive . . . you're impossible. You're not worth wasting any more of my breath! (Stomp, stomp, stomp, slam.)

Art: *Women!? What's the deal? And what did she ever say was wrong with our well?*

How complicated we can make the simplest conversations. We can blow the smallest issues out of proportion. A simple clarification and an understanding of how our minds process information differently could have circumvented many arguments in my marriage.

In recent years, several books have been written to help bridge the gap between the different genders. One by Bill and Pam Farrel is titled, *Men Are Like Waffles, Women Are Like Spaghetti.* In their hilariously insightful explanation of the book's title, they explain men and women in these terms:

Men Are Like Waffles: "We do not mean that men 'waffle' on all decisions and are generally unstable. What we mean is that men process life in boxes. If you look down at a waffle, you see a collection of boxes separated by walls. The boxes are all separate from each other and make convenient holding places. That is typically how a man processes life. Our thinking is divided up into boxes that have room for one issue and one issue only."[1] They continue that men organize every category of their life in separate boxes and like to spend time in the boxes they can succeed in. They have boxes where there are nice thoughts and memories, and other boxes that are blank that have no thoughts or words—thus their ability to tune out at times.

But *Women Are Like Spaghetti:* "In contrast to men's waffle approach, women process life like a plate of pasta. If you look at a plate of spaghetti, you notice that there are lots of individual noodles that all touch one another. If you attempted to follow one noodle around the plate, you would intersect a lot of other noodles, and you might even switch to another noodle seamlessly. This is how women face life. Every thought and issue is connected to every other thought and issue in some way. Life is much more of a process for women than for men."[2]

What great analogies. Now I understand why Art sometimes gets lost in our conversations. I've always misinterpreted his delayed or confused responses as a sign of disinterest. But, according to the Farrels' explanation, that's not the case. On the other hand, I'm sure Art has taken my overload of information at times and, as he bounced from box to box trying to keep up with me, wondered why I can't just get to the bottom line. Yet, even though I now understand a little more about Art's compartmentalized thought life and try to be sensitive to that in our conversations, I'm still like spaghetti. It's the way

I'm wired. Most likely, it's the way your wife is wired too.

Women are sharers. We delight in the journey of conversation from point "A" to point "C" to point "G" and then back to "B." We are seldom looking for quick fixes and solid answers; we just want you to enjoy strolling through our thoughts with us showing true interest. We get offended when you pull out your mental power tools and drill away trying to fix what we consider isn't broken; we just want to share.

In the conversation at the beginning of this chapter, Art should have stopped me when the conversation started bouncing and asked me to clarify. He would have clued in to the correct details and made me feel like he was interested. And I should not have taken his lack of understanding so personally. The best thing to do is ask lots of questions and stay engaged so at least you're on the same page, or plate, as the analogy would have it.

HOME IMPROVEMENT—*Ask your wife to share with you what is on her heart today. Practice the things you've learned from this chapter.*

 THOUGHT FOR THE DAY—*Do not let any unwholesome talk come out of your mouths, but only what is helpful for building others up according to their needs that it may benefit those who listen.*—*[EPHESIANS 4:29]*

CHAPTER 11

TAKE TIME TO COMMUNICATE

I watched to see if what Jenny had shared with me was as severe as she said it was. Sadly, I realized she'd been honest in saying her husband ignored her while at home. Jenny longed for communication, interaction and connection. Her husband, Mike, seemed unaware at best, unconcerned at worst.

Everything in Mike's life revolved around himself. His schedule, his problems at work, his laundry, his meals, his to-do list, and his appointments. Jenny and the kids were left feeling like an afterthought. If they happened to fit in somewhere in his busy life without too much inconvenience, he would put on his family-man hat for short periods of time. This eased the guilt he sometimes felt and put on a good show for friends and neighbors. He rationalized his self-centeredness by saying his role as a husband and father was to be the provider, so he was doing all this for his family's benefit.

What a horrible lie he's bought. What a shame that in the name of "providing" he's set his family on a course headed for destruction. Dr. Ed Wheat, a Christian physician and sex therapist, says, "Husbands should realize that silence presents a negative feedback. As a counselor I have seen how a husband's silence, the seeming indifference to his wife's feelings, and his refusal to discuss things with her can destroy a marriage. It is said, 'Adultery slays its thousands and silence its *ten thousands!*'"[1]

Mike may think silence is a good way to avoid conflict. However, to Jenny, his silence screams, I don't care about you. I wish you weren't here. I'm only staying with you because that is what I'm supposed to do. He wonders why she seems unhappy all the time, why she screams at the kids, and why she is cold to his touches at night. She and the children have become an object of duty rather than the desire and delight of his heart. Mike still gives the token cards on special occasions, sometimes accompanied by a gift or flowers, but they do little to stir Jenny's heart. No woman wants to be the object of duty. John Piper in his book, *Desiring God,* opens with one sentence that illustrates the deadly poison duty infuses into a marriage, "Dutiful roses are a contradiction of terms."

I wish Mike would stop to imagine his life without Jenny and their kids. I've heard people lamenting after the loss of a loved one that they only wished for one more conversation to say things they never took the time to say before. Conversation is priceless, and it's what many wives are longing for from their husbands.

In the surveys I collected, women pleaded for their husbands to take time out of their busy schedules and spend quality time with them communicating. Here are a few of their comments:

■ "Women need to be listened to and nurtured every day."

71

■ "The most important thing a man should know to keep a woman happy is to listen and hold her."

■ "Women live to share everything."

■ "Talk more."

■ "Please listen to what I am saying."

In his book, *Love Life for Every Married Couple,* Dr. Wheat gives practical advice to men who are struggling to communicate and understand their wives. He says, "Husband, this means giving your wife your full, undivided attention so that she feels without question that she is completely loved; that she is valuable enough in her own right to warrant your appreciation and regard."[2] He suggests the following ways to implement focused attention in your relationship:

■ Spend time together alone—really listening to your wife because you want to understand her better. Of course this means the television will be turned off.

■ Look at your wife and move in close to her while you are talking.

■ Plan for times where you will be uninterrupted and then give her the gift of your interested attention.

■ Arrange longer periods for this so that both of you can warm up, let defenses down that may have been temporarily erected, and feel free to share your inmost selves.

■ Pay attention to your wife when other people are around. This will mean more to her than you can ever know.[3]

When I'm sharing with Art and he gets that "you're losing me in the details" look in his eyes, I feel cheated and misinterpret his actions as disinterest in something I've waited all day to share with him. Usually this happens when he comes home with a task in mind other than talking with me. Because he's a task-oriented person, if he's got mowing the lawn on his mind, my abundant conversation is a hindrance to his getting the task checked off his list. The more I press him to converse with me, the more he feels pushed and bothered. No good communication can come from this cycle.

Art and I have learned the importance of setting aside a specified time each day to communicate. We do this after the kids are in bed and the house is quiet. We've stopped watching TV, because it was stealing time for us to connect one-on-one. Now instead of mindlessly watching the tube, we gaze into each other's eyes and engage in meaningful conversation. Art has learned how to be a wonderful listener. This makes me feel important and special.

HOME IMPROVEMENT—*Pray with a sincere heart asking God to infuse your heart with a desire to learn to better connect and communicate with your wife:*

> *Lord, I confess that I have not given the time, attention, and priority to communicating with my wife that I should. By faith I now make a decision to turn things around, to make conversation with her a priority, to risk some things with her because I made promises and took vows that I would love her. This is how I love her—by giving her my time, by talking and listening to her. To recapture the romance of our marriage I pledge myself to lay down my life for my wife. I will make whatever adjustments are needed to be there for her, as she has been there for me. Empower me by your Spirit to keep my commitment. Amen.*

 THOUGHT FOR THE DAY—*Women's needs change all the time. Communicate with your wife often and ask her what she needs.*—MARY [SPRINGFIELD]

CHAPTER 12

A LANGUAGE ALL HER OWN

How many times have you heard your wife say she's told you something, and for the life of you, you can't recall ever hearing her say that? How many times has your wife gotten upset over something but you have no clue why? When you ask her about it she says, "Oh never mind!" as she stomps off? Well, I'm about to reveal a major secret to you: wives have a language all their own. It's called *hints*. We enjoy speaking in *hints* and feel frustrated when husbands don't understand the meaning behind what we are saying.

What is this *hints* language, you ask? *Hints* is a way for a wife to tell her husband something without coming out and saying it. Why would she want to do that? Because if she comes right out and says it, it ruins the outcome she desires. For example, if your wife says to you, "I'm a little stressed out about Thursday. I've got a doctor's appointment, and I can't find anyone to watch Suzie." You might react by suggesting a few people she should ask or by telling her to reschedule. But what she's hinting to you is, "Will you take a late lunch and watch Suzie for me while I go to the doctor on Thursday?" What she wants to know is, in a bind are you willing to go the extra mile for her?

She uses hints because she wants it to be your idea. She's clueing you in on something that you could do that would mean a lot to her. If you don't understand her hint and don't offer to help her, the next time you're having a heated discussion she'll remind you of the time she asked you to watch Suzie for her and you said no. You won't have a clue as to what she's referring to. Thus a breakdown in communication and another argument where you are left scratching your head wondering why women are so complicated.

Instead of being frustrated, why not get intentional about trying to better understand your wife? There are three keys to understanding this hints language:

1. BE PROACTIVE ABOUT FINDING OUT HER NEEDS AND DESIRES

Whether you realize it or not, your wife is constantly speaking in hints. For example, "I wish someone would unload the dishwasher," or "Boy, it sure would be great to get dressed up and go to a nice restaurant sometime," or "My most dreaded chore is putting gas in my car." Become a student of your wife and take notes on what she says. Use these notes to help you decipher her hints. If you're stumped, ask her best friend what your wife has been wishing you would do lately; chances are she will know.

2. TAKE THIS LEARNING PROCESS ONE DAY AT A TIME AND FIND FUN AND ADVENTURE IN IT

I was discussing hints with a friend and her husband, when he got an overwhelmed look on his face. He said he felt like trying to understand women was like climbing a mountain where there were no plateaus. Every time he felt like he was finally getting close to understanding his wife, he'd get to the top of one mountain only to discover another mountain to climb. Take heart. God made us for adventure and the thrill of the challenge, so pursue that woman of yours with a new perspective—not as an impossible mountain but a thrill. Think of how dull it would be if there were no new things to discover about that beautiful bride of yours. Her heart is wonderfully wild and waiting for you to capture it.

3. WHEN IN DOUBT, ASK

No one understands your wife's needs and desires better than she, so why not ask her? Make it a habit to ask her once a week, "Is there anything I could do to make your life sweeter or easier this week?" Sometimes she'll say yes and other times she'll say no, but she will be delighted that you thought enough of her to ask.

Dr. Gary Smalley says the secret to a fulfilling marriage is, "Persistence! Sometimes in the middle of a conflict with Norma, I really want to give up. But that's only how I feel. Often I'm tired, run down, under too much stress—

consequently, the future looks bleak. That's when I rely upon knowledge, not feelings. I act upon what will strengthen our relationship, and in a few days I see the results. In fact, I usually feel better the next day and have a renewed desire to work on our marriage. So I never give up. I keep on acting on what I've learned from the Bible are the secrets of lasting relationships."[1]

I know hints might seem silly and confusing, but like Gary Smalley said, "persistence" is the secret to a fulfilling marriage. Press on and persevere like the great knights so long ago who were determined to rescue their damsels in distress. While your lady may not be physically locked up in a tower, her heart may be behind a wall of self-protection. She longs to have you scale that wall and tell her it's worth it—her heart is worth the inconveniences and pains that are sometimes necessary to reach it. How sweet it is to climb over that wall, touch her heart, and hear her say, "You heard me, you heard my cries for help, and you came for me, my beloved; you are here!"

HOME IMPROVEMENT—*Listen for your wife's hints today. Write them down and try to decipher what her heart is calling out for.*

THOUGHT FOR THE DAY—*Every husband needs to know that no matter what we say, all wives really want is more of them. Not their time but their attention. Not their money but their treasure . . . their hand, their help, and their heart.*—ANONYMOUS

*Your wife needs
her friends and
needs you to allow
her time with the girls,
but ultimately she
wants you to be her
best friend.*

CHAPTER 13

WOMEN NEED TIME
WITH OTHER WOMEN

There are some things only God can give your wife. There are some things only you, as her husband, can give her. There are also things that only friendships with other women can give her. A woman needs all these relationships in her life. At Proverbs 31 Ministry, we have seven principles that we encourage and equip women to follow. Principle number six is: The Proverbs 31 woman speaks with wisdom and faithful instruction as she mentors other women and develops godly friendships.

Building relationships with others and developing godly friendships takes time. While women seem to connect with other women faster than men connect with men, it still takes time to nurture and grow these relationships. My husband is a big fan of my developing friendships with godly women, because he knows he's the direct beneficiary of what I learn. We swap recipes, decorating tips, cleaning ideas, romance ideas, disciplining strategies, and hundreds of other things. Honestly, there are days when I feel discouraged in being a wife and a mom, not because I don't love my family but because I get weary. I am refreshed by spending time with other women, comparing notes, swapping stories, and encouraging each other to press on.

Woman-to-woman relationships are built around women's Bible study groups, meeting for coffee, shopping, decorating together, going out for dinner, and many other ways. But all require time. What a precious gift you can give your wife to allow her time with the girls. In the book I wrote with Sharon Jaynes titled *Seven Life Principles for Every Woman,* I share this story:

A carpenter who was known for his beautiful craftsmanship spent his life building exquisite homes. He paid great attention to the details of his work. When it came time for him to retire, his boss asked if he would build one last home as a special favor.

The carpenter reluctantly agreed. Never had his tired hands ached so as he once again sawed and hammered. His heart was no longer in his job. He rushed through his work, using inferior materials and paying little attention to detail. *No one will probably even notice,* he reasoned. He just wanted to get on with enjoying his retirement.

Finally the house was completed. But his boss had one last request—for the carpenter to meet him at the house to sign some final papers. When they met, the boss shocked the carpenter by handing him the keys to the house, his retirement gift. Oh, if only he had known, he would have done his best work.

So it is with us. Every day we choose our lumber and nails, as we build our lives. If we build wisely, we establish friendships and mentoring relationships that will endure.

However, if we use haphazard methods and just enough effort to make do, we'll never experience the full richness of those relationships.

One day our master carpenter will ask to meet with us. He'll hand us the keys to the eternal home we've built. Will the structure be strong and solid from years of building into others' lives? Will there be timbers of generosity and nails of love that hold up our structure?[1]

God made us to need others—women need other women, who understand the pulls and strains as well as the joys and triumphs of trying to be godly wives and mothers. God created us to build relationships where we give and receive encouragement from our own unique experiences. These friendships are highly personal and greatly prized. Won't you give your wife time to find this treasure?

HOME IMPROVEMENT—*Ask your wife when she would like to schedule a girls' night out with her friends. Tell her you would like to write it on your calendar so you can watch the kids.*

 THOUGHT FOR THE DAY—*Understand that a wife needs her relationship with God, her husband, and family as well as her girlfriends. Give her time to nurture and grow.*
—*AMBER [CHARLOTTE]*

CHAPTER 14

HELP YOUR WIFE FIND HER "ME"

Every woman has dreams that God has placed in her heart. For some seasons of her life, these dreams are placed on the shelf to focus on nurturing a new marriage or a new baby. But when God places a dream in a heart, it's more than chasing after a star, it's a divine calling. Sometimes the calling is to home school her children. Sometimes, like the Proverbs 31 woman, it's to operate a business out of her home. Other times it's to be involved with a ministry in her church. My calling was to serve with the Proverbs 31 Ministry.

My first priorities remained God, my marriage, and my children, but there was a tug at my heart to serve in a ministry for women. Art and I worked on a realistic schedule for the amount of time I could serve. During the day I use the time my children are at school. If I have a meeting or a speaking engagement at night or on the weekend, he tries to be available to help with the kids. Through the years, I have continued to seek Art's counsel on how much time I can give to writing, speaking, and serving in the ministry. He has been supportive, and his willingness to allow me to pursue this calling has meant so much.

I love being his wife. I love being a mommy. But I also love being me: a child of God whom He has called to make a difference in the lives of other women. I can't tell you how much joy it has brought to my heart to know Art believes in me. In preparation for writing this chapter, I asked Art why he's so willing to help me fulfill my calling. This is what he said:

"At first I did it out of obligation. Then, as God grew me, I did it out of a desire to see God use you. I've seen how fulfilled you are in doing what God has called you to do, and I'm the direct benefactor of a happy wife. I'd challenge any husband who wants to be a great husband that if he's not pursuing a way of adding value to his wife by allowing her to pursue her God-given purpose, then he's missing the boat. You've got to help pave the road for her to pursue the dream God has placed in her heart."

One of my greatest treasures is a letter Art wrote to me a couple of years ago while we were attending a Family Life Conference:

Dear Lysa,

From the first day I met you, I can remember how beautiful I thought you were. Your ability to smile at even my bad jokes made me feel special and needed. I love the way you live each day to dream and seek the road ahead with passion. I also love your genuine interest in me and what I do each day. These are the qualities that drew me to you.

After we married and worked through the first year, I was amazed at your willingness to take the lemons of our life and make lemonade. You allowed God to make you so transparent to others and it's simply incredible. Look how He's used your lemons! Proverbs 31 Ministry has been the incubator for a God-sized movement in you. What a joy it is to watch this as your husband. Love, Art

It's been a process. It's amazing that God would call me to serve in a ministry to encourage other women, especially with a ministry called Proverbs 31. If you would have read that Scripture and looked at my life all those years ago, I was nothing like her. I hardly knew how to clean a home much less run it efficiently. I'm not a seamstress, I gave my husband few reasons to sing my praises, and my children were not old enough to rise up much less call me blessed. (See Proverbs 31:10–31 if you're not familiar with this amazing woman.)

But God doesn't call the qualified; He qualifies the called. God used Art's encouragement and patience to help me find the "me" in my life. This "me" loves being a wife, loves being a mommy, loves running an efficient home, and feels fulfilled in serving God through all these things—and through working with the Proverbs 31 Ministry.

What dreams has God placed on your wife's heart?

HOME IMPROVEMENT—*Ask your wife what dreams God has placed on her heart. Record her response here.*

_____

_____

_____

_____

_____

_____

_____

_____

_____

_____

_____

If she has a hard time answering this question, a recommended resource for her to read is a book I wrote to help women with this question: Living Life on Purpose: Discovering God's Best for Your Life *(Moody Press).*

 THOUGHT FOR THE DAY—*He needs to know who I am and what makes me tick. Know my gifts and heart's desires in order to encourage me to be all that God created me to be so I'll have a sense of fulfillment and worth. Know what brings me joy and frustration.*—LAURA [ST. LOUIS]

CHAPTER 15

BECOME YOUR WIFE'S BEST FRIEND

I like skim milk; he likes whole milk. I like to drive the speed limit and stop on yellow lights. He reads speed limit signs with a plus-ten safe zone: if it says fifty-five, it's safe to drive sixty-five; he sees a yellow light as an indication to speed up and beat that red. I like to make a road trip a journey; I enjoy stopping along the way. He likes to set the stopwatch and feels like a failure if we don't beat our last trip's time. I like hot chocolate; he likes coffee. I like to shop; he likes to hunt, even in a store. I like mornings; he likes evenings. I like to be impulsive and last minute; he likes to have things scheduled a month in advance. I love creativity in my organizational efforts; he likes well-maintained order. I like him; he likes me.

Amazing how two creatures can be vastly different and yet wildly attracted to one another. If kept in the right perspective, these differences serve to enhance and add wonder and excitement to a relationship. Why is it that after the honeymoon wears off many couples look up from their cereal bowl and with a disappointed frown, wonder what ever attracted them to each other? At what point along love's journey did they exchange commitment for complacency? How can a couple hold tightly to each other through all life throws at them? I believe the answer lies in friendship.

There was a time in my marriage where Art and I lost sight

of our friendship. We grew distant. He was wrapped up in his work, and I had little ones who kept me more than busy. We fought about little things and never found time to discuss big things. We drifted apart, losing the connection that once held us together as true companions and settled for coexisting. A coldness settled over us. The cords of love that had once held us so tightly were coming unraveled.

My attempts to fix things centered around trying to fix Art. My words were like arrows to his heart. I accused him. I nagged him. I presented long lists of things he was doing wrong. I ranted. I raved. I threatened. Finally, I decided on the ultimate arrow, silence. But my silence wasn't the good kind of quiet; it was filled with bitter thoughts and angry glances.

Art, like a wounded animal, began to retreat farther and farther from me. When we did speak, Art used words that hurt me as much as I'd hurt him. We were caught in a vicious, ugly cycle. Patrick Morley says, "Hurtful words are like poison-tipped arrows that have left the archer's bow: Once they are in the air, they cannot be retrieved."[1]

One day as I prayed for God to fix Art, a thought pierced my conscience: *What if he isn't the one who needs to be fixed?* I brushed aside that thought, as I recalled a list of hurtful things he'd said to me lately, but the thought wouldn't leave me. Not long after that I read Ephesians 4:29–32, which says, "Do not let any unwholesome talk come out of your mouths, but only what is helpful for building others up according to their needs, that it may benefit those who listen. And do not grieve the Holy Spirit of God, with whom you were sealed for the day of redemption. Get rid of all bitterness, rage and anger, brawling and slander, along with every form of malice. Be kind and compassionate to one another, forgiving each other, just as in Christ God forgave you."

That sent my head spinning. God was calling me to be the one to wave the white surrender flag and walk back to my husband's side. Not only was I grieving my mate, I was grieving the Holy Spirit of God. Wasn't it my right to hold on to a quest seeking vengeance for the ways Art had hurt me? Absolutely not. I had to let it go and forgive as Christ had forgiven me. I had to look for ways to build him up according to his needs, and I had to let go of the bitterness.

God is calling you to be the one today to stand tall, wave the white flag, and walk back to your wife's side. Let go of the fighting, let go of the past, let go of your right to be right, and ask her for forgiveness. Ask her to forgive you for all the times you put other things ahead of her. Ask her to forgive you for being selfish and inconsiderate. Ask her to forgive you for seeking revenge instead of seeking forgiveness. Tell her you want to be her best friend. Ask her to show you how.

Despite all the ways you differ, marriage can be wonderful when mates hold on to the strong similarity in their desire to be best friends. I still like skim milk; Art still likes whole milk. I still like to drive the speed limit and stop on yellow lights; he still reads speed limit signs with a plus-ten safe zone! I still like to make a road trip like a journey; he still likes to set the stopwatch. I still like hot chocolate; he still likes coffee. I still like to shop; he still likes to hunt. I still like mornings; he still likes evenings. I still like to be impulsive; he still likes to have things scheduled. I still love creativity; he still likes order. I still like him; he still likes me.

HOME IMPROVEMENT—*Write five things you could do to foster your friendship with your wife.*

_____

_____

_____

_____

 THOUGHT FOR THE DAY—*The best thing my husband ever said to me was that I was his best friend.*—*JENNY [BLOOMINGTON]*

Your wife needs you

to be a "triple A"

encourager by giving

her appreciation,

affirmation, and

admiration.

CHAPTER 16

HOW TO BUILD YOUR WIFE'S SELF-ESTEEM

No matter how beautiful a woman is, she will struggle with not liking something about herself. No matter how confident a woman seems, insecurities still haunt her at times. No matter how fulfilled a woman is in her calling in life, there will always be a part of her that wonders if she measures up. Some women struggle more than others, but all women long to be affirmed, appreciated, and admired. Other than God, there's no one who can do more to build a woman's self-esteem than her husband.

What if I told you that your wife is in the process of becoming what you think of her? If you cut her down, lose your temper with her, and constantly remind her of her shortcomings thus making her feel like an ogre, then an ogre she'll be. If you think of her as the most beautiful treasure God has given you and affirm her through your actions and words, soon the most amazing woman you've ever seen will grace the halls of your home and call you her beloved husband.

Never have I seen this illustrated more clearly than through the story of Johnny Lingo and his eight-cow wife. Johnny Lingo was known as a clever businessman in his South Pacific island home. Even neighboring islands knew of this man and his ability to acquire the best quality goods at the best prices. So rumors flew when Johnny Lingo paid the unheard of price of eight cows for a woman named Sarita, whom many described as less than attractive.

As one person recalls, this is how the legend goes . . .

I knew enough about the island customs to be thoroughly impressed. Two or three cows would buy a fair-to-middling wife; four or five a highly satisfactory one.

"Eight cows!" I said. She must be a beauty who takes your breath away."

"The kindest could only call Sarita plain," was Shenkin's [a guest house manager] answer. "She was skinny. She walked with her shoulders hunched and her head ducked. She was scared of her own shadow."

"Then how do you explain the eight cows?"

"We don't," he said. "And that's why the villagers grin when they talk about Johnny. They get special satisfaction from the fact that Johnny, the sharpest trader in the islands, was bested by Sarita's father, dull old Sam Karoo."

"Eight cows," I said unbelievingly. "I'd like to meet this Johnny Lingo."

So the next afternoon I sailed a boat to Nurabandi and met Johnny at his home, where I asked about his eight-cow purchase of Sarita. I assumed he had done it for his own vanity and reputation—at least until Sarita walked into the room. She was the most beautiful woman I have ever seen. The lift of her shoulders, the tilt of her chin, the sparkle of her eyes all spelled a pride to which no one could deny her the right.

I turned back to Johnny Lingo after she left.

"You admire her?" he asked.

"She . . . She's glorious," I said. "But she's not the Sarita from Kiniwata."

"There's only one Sarita. Perhaps she does not look the way they say she looked in Kiniwata."

"She doesn't." The impact of the girl's appearance made me forget my tact. "I heard she was homely. They all make fun of you because you let yourself get cheated by Sam Karoo."

"You think eight cows were too many?" A smile slid over his lips.

"No. But how can she be so different?"

"Do you ever think," he asked, "what it must mean to a woman to know that her husband settled on the lowest price for which she could be bought? And then later, when the women talk, they boast of what their husbands paid for them. One says four cows; another maybe six. How does she feel, the woman who was sold for one or two? This could not happen to my Sarita."

"Then you did this just to make her happy?" I asked.

"I wanted Sarita to be happy, yes. But I wanted more than that. You say she is different. This is true. Many things change a woman. Things that happen inside and things that happen outside. But the thing that matters most is what she thinks about herself. In Kiniwata, Sarita believed she was worth nothing. Now she knows she is worth more than any other woman on the islands."

"Then you wanted . . ."

"I wanted to marry Sarita. I loved her and no other woman."

"But . . ."

"But," he finished softly, "I wanted an eight-cow wife."[1]

HOME IMPROVEMENT—*Start a list of things you find incredible about your wife. Keep it in your Bible and add to it often. After you've compiled thirty or so items, frame the list (written in your handwriting) and give it to your wife on what would otherwise seem like an ordinary day. Soon you, too, will have an eight-cow wife.*

 THOUGHT FOR THE DAY—*Every wife needs to believe that her husband truly sees her as the most beautiful woman in the world.*—MIRIAM [EUREKA]

CHAPTER 17

THE WAY TO YOUR WIFE'S HEART

Ashley came bouncing into the bathroom where I was bathing her baby sister. She beamed, as with great pleasure she threw down a yardstick to which she'd tied a black ribbon and extended it to the center of her little six-year-old forehead. "Look, Mommy," she proudly exclaimed. "I'm taller than this string, and I have a new rule. Anyone who comes over to our house to visit that is as tall as this string gets a piece of candy."

I was careful with my answer. Ashley is shorter than most kids her age. At times this has caused her distress, especially when friends and older sister get to ride certain rides at the local amusement park that she is deemed too short to ride. Gently I took the string and yardstick from Ashley and held her sweet little face. "Ashley, I like your new rule that whoever is as tall as the string gets *a* piece of candy but I'd like to add to it. Whoever is not as tall as this string gets *two* pieces of candy. You see, darling, how tall a person stands is not determined by her height but rather her heart. You have a sweet heart, so you stand very tall in my eyes and even more importantly in God's eyes." She smiled and ran back to her little girl world of baby dolls and princess dresses, leaving the measuring stick behind.

Inside every big girl is a little girl who, like Ashley, wonders, "Do I measure up?" Every week at the grocery store she stands in line while the perfectly airbrushed pictures of skinny models and movie stars bombard her. She looks at her tummy that's gotten a little rounder with each pregnancy. She bites her lip as she thinks about the upcoming swimsuit season and having to face her less-than-muscular thighs. Sometimes without realizing it she throws down that measuring stick, stretches that string, and quietly wonders.

She's wondered it since she was little when she twirled and danced in front of her daddy and cried, "Look, Daddy, look. Am I beautiful? Am I pretty? Do you notice me?" She threw down her little measuring stick and according to her daddy's reaction stretched the string and quietly wondered. She wondered it in junior high when boys were starting to notice girls. Though she felt awkward and unsure, she joined in the game. She threw down her measuring stick, stretched the string, and wondered. Suddenly it was time for others to vote for homecoming queen, time for high school sweethearts, prom dates, college applications and class rankings. She threw down her measuring stick, stretched the string, and wondered. And she's been wondering ever since.

Chances are the longer she's a Christian and the closer she grows to the Lord, she'll pull out that stick less and less. While her comparison to others may ease up a bit, the wondering in her heart is still a constant battle. Even when she knows in her head that God loves her and calls her beautiful, her heart still longs to be desired by a man . . . her man . . . you. She wants to know she is beautiful, because she's heard it spill from your lips and felt it in your touch. She wants to know that you find her absolutely captivating, worth fighting for, worth living for.

John Eldredge, in his book *Wild at Heart,* says,

> Listen to the longing of a woman's heart: she wants to be more than noticed—she wants to be wanted. She wants to be pursued . . . and every woman wants an adventure to share [where she is fought for] . . .
>
> And finally, every woman wants to have a beauty to unveil. Not to conjure but to unveil. Most women feel the pressure to be beautiful from very young, but that is not what I speak of. There is also a deep desire to simply and truly be the beauty and be delighted in.[1]

Sadly John goes on to contrast these desires with what many women feel in reality: "No one is fighting for her heart; there is no grand adventure to get swept up in; and every woman doubts very much that she has any beauty to unveil."[2]

King Solomon knew the way to a woman's heart was through her ears. He knew how to break that measuring stick once and for all. When his beloved says, "I am a rose of Sharon, a lily of the valleys" in Song of Solomon 2:1, she is basically saying I am just a common flower, one among many. To which he replies in verse 2, "Like a lily among thorns is my darling among the maidens." In other words he says, "Oh, no, you are extraordinary and rare. You don't even compare; your worth is exceeding."

Look at her twirling about you. Can you almost see it on

her face? *Do you notice me? Am I your princess? Am I your beauty? Do I captivate you? Is my heart worth fighting for?* That's the question on your wife's heart. What answer will she hear?

HOME IMPROVEMENT—*Write your wife a note today and stick it in her wallet where she will find it. Tell her she is extraordinary and rare.*

 THOUGHT FOR THE DAY—*Like a lily among thorns is my darling among the maidens.*—[SONG OF SOLOMON 2:2]

CHAPTER 18

RECRUITING THE WARRIOR
WHO FIGHTS FOR HER

I hate getting the oil changed in my car, and I despise taking my car in once a year for an inspection North Carolina requires. Last year I kept putting the inspection off. When I finally went, they informed me I owed a huge fine. There I was crying in the middle of a greasy car garage with small children in tow, because unless I paid the unreasonable fine, I couldn't get my car inspected. The longer I waited to have it inspected, the higher the fine would get.

My tears weren't just about the inspection, or even the fine, it was that I felt helpless. No one cared that I had small children, and it was difficult for me to bring them into this dirty place and wait for an unreasonable amount of time. There was no mercy or grace extended, just "pay us the fine and get out of our face." Rule-follower that I am, I had gone to get the car inspected once before during the appropriate time but had been turned down because something wasn't right with some gauge or light or some other engine part that was foreign to me. Then life had gotten busy, and I forgot to go back.

By the time it dawned on me, it was past any DMV employee's ability to extend me grace. At first, I calmly tried to reason with them, explaining my dilemma the first time I came to get it inspected. I tried to reason with them with just plain innocence. I honestly did not know there would be such a penalty for a late inspection. Then I started getting upset and tried to plead to their emotions. Nothing helped. They were cold and rude. They could have said that they understood how I could have gotten delayed or even that they were sorry that I had to pay so much, but they didn't.

I paid the fine and thought, *I'll show you . . . just wait until my husband hears how you treated me. He'll be back with a Terminator voice and a Rambo attitude and he'll beat you up, that's what he'll do; he'll, he'll, he'll fight for me.* Though the words didn't come out audibly, just thinking them lifted the gray cloud in my spirit and put a smile back on my tear-streaked face.

Now you might be thinking, *You cried? Over a late fee and a car inspection? You mean your eyes actually produced enough tears over this situation to streak your face? Oh, brother . . . get a life!*

A life . . . a real "someone thinks I'm worth fighting for" life . . . that's why I cried. The ways of a woman's heart are mysterious and deep, and they run over with emotion. To try to understand her is impossible, but to capture and protect her heart is valiant, the call of a true warrior who fights to the bloody end to protect the one he loves.

Remember when you were a boy? The swords and the guns and the hunt for bad guys? Don't forget the thrill of pretending there was blood and guts and gore. You ran; you jumped; you knocked over your mom's favorite lamp to climb to the fortress and take back your land. Was all this just boy's play? No, it was your dress rehearsal for today's curtain call. Your damsel is in distress.

She's being held captive by a world that's told her to be tough, take it on the chin, and show she's as tough as any man. Yet, deep inside she's desiring something more: a tender protector. Gary Smalley, a nationally recognized authority on marriage, suggests that a husband learn to become his wife's tender protector by discovering where she needs protection. Smalley says, "a husband needs to discover areas in which his wife feels vulnerable. Through informal discussions and observation on your part, you can compile mental lists of the major and minor areas where she is frustrated or fearful."[1]

So what keeps many husbands from doing this? It sounds simple. John Eldridge, author of *Wild at Heart,* gives an interesting perspective. "Why don't men offer what they have to their women? Because we know deep down in our guts that it won't be enough. There is an emptiness to Eve after the Fall, and no matter how much you pour into her she will never be filled. This is where so many men falter. Either they refuse to give what they can, or they keep pouring and pouring into her and all the while feel like a failure because she is still needing more. . . . The barrenness of Eve you can never hope to fill. She needs God more than she needs you, just as you need Him more than you need her. So what do you do? Offer what you have. . . . You love her because that's what you are made to do; that's what a real man does."[2]

That day in that smelly old garage, the thing that lifted my overwhelmed heart was knowing I had a warrior at home who'd waited all his life to defend me. Soon those people at the DMV would hear the hooves of his stallion (okay, okay, the tires of his Ford Explorer) beating the path in their direction. And he did. No, Art didn't go back that day and beat everyone up. No, he didn't set out to fix my insecurities and teach me how to be tough. He simply gave me the money for the fine without any chastisement. This year when it was time for the inspection, guess who went? My warrior. My hero. My protector.

HOME IMPROVEMENT—*Ask your wife if there is an area of her life where she feels frustrated or fearful. Then, become her protector.*

 THOUGHT FOR THE DAY—*It's the little things that matter the most. Please take the time to give that hug, kiss, say, "I love you," and tell me it will be okay—that we'll get through this together.*—MONICA [BURBANK]

Your wife needs to

feel emotionally

filled before she

desires to be

sexually involved.

CHAPTER 19

SEX: A MOST CONTROVERSIAL WEDDING GIFT

Sex was on the hearts and minds of the women I surveyed. I received more advice on what men should know about sex than any of the other categories. Sex is God's gift to married couples. He designed it to be a beautiful expression of intimacy between a husband and a wife. However, He designed men and women different in their approach to the marriage bed. I do not want to put all women in a box and say they are all alike. However, the majority of women I talk to struggle with some aspect of the sexual relationship with their husband. For most, it's not that they don't desire a sexual relationship, it's just that sex is more mental for a wife than for a husband. A man can be ready to hop into the bed with one look at his wife. He is stimulated visually. Most women are not visually stimulated. How are women stimulated? Jane from Springfield explains, "A husband that does the dishes and vacuums the floor increases his chances of a sexual encounter by 80 percent."

According to Dennis Rainey, women are stimulated by touch, attitudes, actions, words, and are person-centered. Men are stimulated by sight and smell and are body-centered.[1] This is why men are quickly aroused whereas women need time and attention. Debbie from Sherrard says, "Take the time to get to know me as a person, who I am, what I like, and don't like. Then you will find our sex life will be so much better."

I've heard it said that sex starts in the kitchen. I believe that goes for what a husband does for his wife and what he says to her in every room *except* the bedroom. Once you enter the bedroom, if you suddenly say and do all the right things, you will appear to have an obvious agenda.

Kelly from Tinley Park says, "Every husband should know that cleaning the kitchen or helping with household chores is foreplay." Like it or not, it's the truth. Women need to feel filled emotionally. You fill her emotionally by your attitude, actions, and words. Your wife's desire for you sexually is related to how much she feels loved, cherished, and appreciated. Lori from Altoona explains, "A woman needs to feel emotionally attached before she has the desire to feel physically connected with her husband."

Now that you know what stimulates your wife, let's turn our attention to frequency. In *Intimate Issues* authors Dillow and Pintus, tell of a scene from a movie that shows a husband and wife each talking with a therapist. The man complains, "We hardly ever have sex. Maybe three times a week, tops." The woman laments, "We are constantly having sex. We must have it three times a week."[2] This dialogue is consistent with the age-old tension between husbands and wives.

One night my husband and I were having this "frequency" discussion. I was trying to help him understand that just because I did not want to make love at times did not mean I did not love him. I explained that as a mother of young children I am on touch-overload by the time I go to bed. I have been touched all day long, so by the time I crawl into bed, I only have sleep on my mind. It's as if I were full, and someone placed my favorite dish in front of me. I am simply too full to partake. Art listened, then he painted his own version of this word picture. He had not had anything to eat in several days and was close to being famished. Then someone placed his favorite meal in front of him but instructed him he must only look, not touch or partake.

 How can we resolve this? Well, you need to learn how to make your wife hungry. She will only long for you sexually if she feels filled emotionally. I can't tell you what to say to fill your wife emotionally. This is something you need to discover by getting to know her unique desires. I can, however, give you a little insight on getting started.

This is the story of two real people whose names have been changed to protect their identity, but I imagine some version of this has taken place in your home. Dan and Linda have been married for seven years and have three children, ages four, two, and ten months. Dan travels with his job and is gone at least three nights a week. When Dan is gone, Linda is responsible for every detail of life within their home, which leaves her feeling exhausted and spent. When Dan returns home, he is ready to be intimate with his wife. Linda wants to please her husband and meet his needs but resents his lack of communication and affection before they get into bed. You see, Linda is full. Dan needs to help Linda get hungry.

One of the best ways to do this is to acknowledge how challenging it was to take care of the house and children solo for three days. Ask her how things have gone. Admire the great job she has done and tell her you think she is an incredible wife and mother. Now Linda is hungry enough for an appetizer.

Next, recognize her need for downtime and allow her to do something just for her. Maybe she'd like a bubble bath, time to paint her nails, or time to read a chapter in a book. Offer to put the kids to bed and give her this time. Now Linda is starting to get her appetite back.

Lastly, tell Linda you love her and thought of her often while you were gone. Tell her you missed being close to her and couldn't wait to get home to hold her in your arms once again. Be patient with her response and don't expect her to be instantly transformed into the sex goddess of your dreams. If she responds sexually, great. If she does not, do not ruin all you have done by acting frustrated and angry. Go to bed and sleep. Sleep may be what Linda needs more than anything. The next day, keep lovingly investing your energies in her, and she will eventually respond. When she does, tell her she is a beautiful lover and hold her for as long as she wants.

If you treat your wife this way, you will fill her emotionally, and unless there are extenuating circumstances chances are the frequency issue will resolve itself. Darla from Sedalia says, "If you make your wife your number one priority behind God and if she feels secure in that, your needs will be met."

HOME IMPROVEMENT—*Ask your wife how she likes to be emotionally filled. You may also want to ask her how you can become her dream lover. You may be surprised at her answer.*

 THOUGHT FOR THE DAY—*Emotional and spiritual intimacy lead to sexual intimacy. I need to feel close in these ways to feel close in other ways.*—STACY [NEOGA]

CHAPTER 20

GREET "SEX"PECTATIONS

James Dobson, founder of Focus on the Family, said, "Some would say, 'having sex' and 'making love' are one and the same, but there's an important distinction between the two. The physical act of intercourse can be accomplished by any appropriately matched mammals, as well as most other members of the animal kingdom. But the art of making love, as designed by God, is a much more meaningful and complex experience—it's physical, emotional, and spiritual. In marriage we should settle for nothing less than a sexual relationship that is expressed not only body to body, but heart to heart and soul to soul."[1]

It's easy to understand how to connect with your wife body-to-body. Like the song goes, "Just doin' what comes naturally." Understanding how to connect heart-to-heart and soul-to-soul is more challenging. These deeper connections are not only possible but essential in binding two whom God joined together inseparably.

The great "sex"pectations of our society constantly flash the message that being connected body-to-body with another is all about the pleasure that can be gained through the encounter. What if we viewed it as something much more meaningful? For your wife, making love is not an encounter, it is an experience. It's not something that is turned on for thirty minutes and off for the other twenty-four and a half hours of the day. For her "experience" to be complete, she needs you to set the stage for making love by connecting with her heart-to-heart and soul-to-soul throughout the day.

Before you start rolling your eyes and shaking your head, think back to the days before you were married, before you connected body-to-body. Remember the thrill of discovery? The days when you laid the foundation of your relationship by connecting heart-to-heart? Finding out her favorite foods, what makes her happy, dreams for her future, and hopes for her tomorrows. She still wants you to share these things with her, only now on a deeper level. No longer are they just her dreams, she wants her desires to be your dreams too. And she wants you to share goals and aspirations that are tucked away in your heart, as well.

One of the most meaningful times of my marriage was when Art made my passion for writing and dream of being a published author, a dream he could dream with me. How thrilled I was to catch him reading my manuscripts not because I asked him to but because he wanted to. How fun it's been for me to see "our" dreams become a reality. And, oh, how attracted I am to him when he tells me how proud he is of me. When we connect heart-to-heart, I desire to be connected body-to-body.

I also want to connect soul-to-soul with Art. Recently we determined that this area of our marriage needed to be worked on, so we decided to make it a priority to do a nightly devotion in our bed before we turn out the lights. This has been a wonderful way to melt away the stress of our day and soften any quarrels and petty arguments we may have had earlier. Reading a couple's devotional book or God's Word and praying together gives us a fresh perspective and helps connect us in that deeper soul level. There's something about our home at night when the kids are in bed and we are alone reading, talking, sharing, and praying that has made our relationship incredibly intimate.

Why not take an inventory of your intimate relationship with your wife and together answer these questions:

■ What is the difference between having sex and making love?

■ Is there anything about our intimate life that could be improved upon?

■ How can we better connect heart-to-heart?

■ What are your dreams for the future?

■ Do we regularly connect soul-to-soul?

■ How could we make connecting soul-to-soul a priority?

■ Is there anything I need to seek your forgiveness for in this area of our lives?

■ What do you love most about our marriage?

These are not the kinds of questions you fly through at the breakfast table while wolfing down coffee and toast. Let me encourage you to set aside some time to get away with your wife where the two of you can be alone and uninterrupted. If finances are tight, get creative. Pack a picnic lunch and go to a quiet park in your area. If you can afford to get away overnight, trade baby-sitting with another couple or ask Grandma and Grandpa if they'd like time with their grandkids.

Art and I discovered a wonderful bed-and-breakfast that we steal away to a couple of times a year to have these types of discussions. There are no TVs, just beautifully piped-in music and lots of time for sweet conversation and connection. We leave the ups and downs of life behind as we escape to a little place we are sure must be a little like heaven. We schedule our special time in advance and determine that no matter what deadlines might be pressuring us to delay or cancel our trip, we don't forgo this investment in our marriage.

HOME IMPROVEMENT—*Plan a date to connect and discuss the questions from this chapter.*

 THOUGHT FOR THE DAY—*Oh, how attracted I am to him when he tells me how proud he is of me. When we connect heart-to-heart, I desire to be connected body-to-body.*—[LYSA TERKEURST]

CHAPTER 21

ROMANCE 101

I thought you might enjoy hearing from my husband, Art, on the delicate subject of romance. So without further ado, here's Art spelling out the basics of romance . . . LOVE.

LOOK AT YOUR SPOUSE IN A NEW LIGHT

First Peter 3:7 says, in essence, "Husband live with your wife in an understanding way, thoughtful of her needs and honoring her. Remember that you and your wife are partners in receiving God's blessings." Husbands, we need to get behind our wives' eyes and see life the way they do. Romancing her needs to be an intentional act, especially in today's wide-open fifth-gear society.

First Corinthians 7:3 in *The Message* says, "Marriage is a decision to serve the other whether in bed or out." While a husband desires to be loved and served inside the bed, the woman desires to be served and loved outside the bed. God made us different for a reason, and it's our job to find out how we can romance our wives in the middle of our everyday hectic schedules.

Not too long ago my wife and friend gave me a package of five golf lessons. The first three were on the range with the golf pro. One was with a video and another was application on the course. I learned more on the first day with the pro than anything else. He taught me how to stand over the ball, how to better grip the club, and the importance of where the club face is from 4–8 o'clock. It improved my game, as long as I remembered to practice and apply what I'd learned. The point is: If we are going to learn how to improve our romantic game with our wives, we have to go to the pro. In this case the pro is our wife. I asked Lysa what can I do to improve in the area of romance and she gave me some helpful tips:

Adore her in public and in private. King Solomon is Mr. Romantic. In Song of Solomon 7:1–9 he admires his wife's character and her body by using beautiful poetic imagery. Lysa needs to hear me tell her how beautiful she is every day. She needs me to lift her up and encourage her with her dreams. Her dreams need to be my dreams. I let her know how proud and excited I am about the book she is writing or the way she's mothering our kids or caring for our house. It's not natural for me to do these things, so one way to help me remember is to put a little note on my Palm Pilot that reminds me at the top of each day to "encourage Lysa."

OFFER TO HELP

A man's approach to work is single-minded and independent, while a woman's approach is to balance several plates at once while incorporating relationship whenever possible. Let me give you an example. If I were out in the yard, working to get those mowing lines just right, and Lysa came over and said, "Let me help you, honey, and let's talk while we do yard work together," I would feel interrupted and a little agitated. I can't relate and converse while in my "working on the yard" mode. If Lysa is trying to knock out her daily list and I step in and offer to help with the dishes and the vacuuming, her eyes will soften. She'll see me as her knight in shining armor. We may not think it's macho to change diapers and dry dishes, but it's sexy to our wives. If drying dishes counts as foreplay, I'm all for it.

I also have learned the value of helping Lysa fulfill her dreams. For her to fly to speaking engagements and do all that's required in the ministry, I have to help her. I take care of the children and cover all her endeavors in prayer. I no longer see it as a sacrifice. When Lysa is doing what God has created her to do, He fills her. When she is full of God, then she is able to serve our family with a joyful heart. I am convinced a happy wife is a fulfilled wife.

What are your wife's dreams? What could you do to help show her you believe in those dreams? What calling has God placed on your wife? How could you help her fulfill that call?

VALUE HER FEMININITY

Ephesians 5:28–29 instructs: "Husbands ought to love their wives as their own bodies. He who loves his wife loves himself. After all, no one ever hated his own body, but he feeds and cares for it, just as Christ does the church."

Today's society has hardened women, and it's our challenge to appreciate them as the feminine beings God created them to be. A great example came from our good friend King Solomon. He knew how to draw out his wife's best. Song of Solomon 3 tells how Solomon created a processional for his bride, complete with sixty warriors and fully armored soldiers, followed by servants spraying the perfumes and spices, and lastly his bride sitting on a throne made from the finest woods and fabrics. King Solomon knew the importance of wooing, romancing, valuing, adoring, and helping his wife feel feminine.

Ask your wife what you can do to value her femininity. What is it that makes her feel wooed, romanced, valued, and adored?

EXCITE HER SENSES

God gave your wife five senses that when stimulated can make her feel romantic. This came full circle for me about two weeks ago. Lysa and I dropped off our girls with friends, and we slipped out of town for three days. We went to a bed-and-breakfast in the mountains, a place that was a female five-senses home run. There was no TV (so Sportscenter was out of the question), but for Lysa this place was as if she had been "whisked away into a woman's wonder world weekend." For three days I witnessed a transformation in my wife from poopy diapers, dirty dishes, and deadlines to complete softness and relaxation. You'd think after one day the place would get a little old, but it never happened. It was for her as you and I would feel if we were sitting in a new Triton nineteen foot bass boat three days on Lake Okeechobee. Or maybe playing eighteen holes with Tiger Woods at Augusta National the day before the Masters. This wonder world weekend softened Lysa's senses and called forth her femininity, of which I was the happy recipient.

I have learned sex is not an event, it is an environment. It's not an act for my wife, it's an atmosphere. This atmosphere doesn't have to be a weekend away at a bed-and-breakfast, it can be duplicated inside your home. Find out what makes her feel special and pampered and create that for her. Maybe it's relaxing in a warm bath with her favorite book, while candles are burning and soft music is playing. While your wife is pampered there in your own home, you can cap things off by putting the kids down and finish just in time to be the lucky winner of your wife's recharged femininity.

HOME IMPROVEMENT—*Write one thing you know would excite each of your wife's five senses.*

Sight: _____

_____

Sound: _____

_____

Touch: _____

_____

Taste: _____

_____

Smell: _____

_____

 THOUGHT FOR THE DAY—*One compliment a day goes a long way . . . and the compliment only counts if her clothes are on.*—*LISA [MOLINE]*

*Your wife needs
you to understand
that there are some
things you will never
understand. This
doesn't make either of
you right or wrong—
just different.*

CHAPTER 22

"JUST BECAUSE"

Grace looked up from the old, worn photo album to see Richard the postman hastily making his way through the cold to her door. *What a sweet young man,* she thought. Grace loved her walks to the mailbox in late spring and through the summer, but the cold November air seemed to whip through her thin skin. Though in her heart she still felt like a young, energetic girl, her age was evident to her now. Her aches and pains made her careful and slow. As the air turned cooler, Richard made it a habit to deliver Grace's mail to her door. Grace had never asked, which made the gesture sweeter. *Maybe,* Grace thought, *he's simply captivated by this old woman's beauty.* She smiled. *Or maybe, he's captivated by the cookies I sometimes give him.* Either way, Grace was glad to see him coming.

Today was an especially lonely day for Grace. It was the seventeenth of November. No one but her Jim would have known what a special day this was. It wasn't her birthday or even their anniversary. To all her friends and family, it was just the seventeenth. But to Grace it was their special day. For forty-two years the seventeenth of every month was their special day, as Jim would say, *just because.* Though they never were rich with money, they were determined to be rich with love. For this reason on the seventeenth Jim always found some special way to say it.

Over the years the gifts had been as simple as a scribbled note or as elaborate as a bouquet of store-bought flowers. But the message was always the same: "Just because." Once he'd secretly taken Grace's wedding band from her jewelry box and had it engraved with their special saying. She was almost crazy with grief as she searched the house over only to discover when Jim presented it to her later that evening, it too had become part of the game.

How she found such comfort, confidence, and connection in those two simple words. To Grace it was more than a gesture of love, it was an outward symbol of much more. When she was pregnant with each of their three children, it meant *you are most beautiful when you are so full of life*. When she'd gotten sick and couldn't keep up with the house and cooking, it meant *I love you for who you are not what you do*. When they'd had an argument, it meant *even when we don't see eye-to-eye I love you still*. When she'd started aging, it meant *yours is a timeless beauty*. Though Jim had never been a man of many words, his *just because* was perfect and poetic to Grace.

Jim had passed away three weeks ago. It had not been a sudden death; they both had known his end was near. They'd had a sweet time of reminiscing, hugging, crying, and then as quickly as he came into her life all those years ago, he was gone. She missed him terribly but had a peace about it all. They'd had a wonderful life and left nothing unsaid. Now Grace loved flipping through their old photo albums savoring old pictures, but even more so she loved touching all the mementos from over the years written in his masculine handwriting.

Though she'd seen Richard the postman coming up the walkway, the doorbell startled Grace. Carefully, she laid the old book down and made her way to the door. She graciously took the few letters he handed her and apologized for not having the energy today to make him cookies. Maybe tomorrow. She then walked slowly to the kitchen and sat down at the table to open her mail. A bill, another sympathy card, and then something that made her heart jump and melt all at the same time.

Her eyes filled with tears and her hand trembled as she slid her finger underneath the envelope's back flap. It was a simple letter as they always were, delivered on the seventeenth as they always had been. Jim had, before his death, arranged for Richard to make one last special delivery. "Not even death shall stop my heart. Just because, Jim."

Sometimes a short story can illustrate a point so much better than pages and pages of instruction. This kind of love is what the heart of your beautiful bride longs for. Not flashy but forever; not commercial but committed. Let this story settle into your heart and reveal something more about the tender, expectant heart of your beloved. She's waited all her life to hear you say something simple, yet profound: *I love you, just because.*

HOME IMPROVEMENT—*Write your wife a simple note to say you love her just because.*

 THOUGHT FOR THE DAY—*But the greatest of these is love.—[1 CORINTHIANS 13:13]*

CHAPTER 23

PMS IS FOR REAL

A rt is a manly man who would have loved to have had a house full of boys. However, God had a different plan for our family, and we have a house full of girls. Girls who, I must add, have stolen my husband's heart and in whom he delights every day. There is one thing, however, that has caused Art a little stress about being surrounded by a sea of estrogen. It's the whole hormone thing.

One day we were having a discussion about the girls, and Art asked, "What am I going to do when you are all going through menopause at the same time?" I laughed. I knew what he meant to ask was: What was he going to do when we were having menstrual symptoms at the same time? (In case you don't know, there is a difference.) I explained the difference, and then suggested that when the time comes he get away with his guy friends for a few days each month.

In 1983 Niels H. Lauerson, M.D., and Eileen Stukane wrote a book titled *Premenstrual Syndrome and You*. These words appeared on the cover: "Over five million women are in the dark about a severe hormonal imbalance affecting them 10 days out of every month. They are frightened by the violent fluctuations in mood, depression, and weight gain, and they don't know what's causing them."[1]

Jean Lush, in her book *Women and Stress,* describes the emotional phases a woman goes through using seasons. It is one of the best descriptions of PMS and one worth reading and understanding for both your wife's sake and yours. Here is a summary of what she writes:

PHASE 1: THE SPRING PHASE

This phase starts with the blood flow of the menstrual cycle and is dominated by estrogen. During this time, a woman feels bright and fresh like spring. (This is after the cramps and aches associated with menstruation have stopped.) New surges of life burst inside her. She is positive, assertive, outgoing, happy, energetic, and well coordinated. Little threatens her, and she can accomplish almost anything. Her relationship with her husband and kids is delightful and relaxed. The tension she felt prior to her period vanishes, and life is a whole new ball game.

PHASE 2: THE SUMMER PHASE

This is a peaceful, happy, affirming, creative time of the month. A woman has the "warm fuzzies" for her family and friends and is generally pleased with life. She is a bit less assertive than in the spring phase but able to accomplish much. Her body is moving toward liberating an egg for fertilization. Estrogen continues to dominate.

PHASE 3: THE MIDSUMMER PHASE

Midsummer is that short time during which ovulation occurs. The egg leaves the ovary for possible fertilization. A woman usually feels euphoric, motherly, peaceful, sensual, and integrative. Everything in life seems absolutely wonderful. She loves her husband and kids, who can do no wrong. All of these feelings are influenced by progesterone production.

PHASE 4: THE FALL PHASE

Immediately after ovulation, a woman begins to slowly lose energy as she enters the fall phase. Slight depression or the doldrums set in, and she isn't as enthusiastic about life as she was a few days ago. Suddenly her husband and children don't seem quite so lovable. Assertiveness is a thing of the past, and her confidence is droopy. It is generally suspected that during the fall and winter phases, hormone fluctuations are responsible for a host of unpleasant symptoms.

PHASE 5: THE WINTER PHASE

Winter sets in around the fourth week of the menstrual month, and many women become downright nasty. There are typical symptoms associated with this phase: sluggish, depressed, irritable, weepy, outbursts of emotion, jumpiness, expressed resentment, expressed hostility, suspicious, frustration, sudden mood swings, irrational, supersensitive, abnormally hungry, crying over everything (the list goes on). Fortunately, the menstrual flow is only a few days away and a woman will feel quite different once this begins.[2]

Yes, this whole hormone thing is challenging. It is hard for you to endure, but let me assure you it is no walk in the park for women either. I have wondered if I might be going crazy with all these fluctuations and mood swings. Now, all women are not alike. While these descriptions may apply to the majority, your wife's response to hormonal changes may be different. In any case, though, there will be changes; for most there will be a time of emotional difficulty.

I say this not to scare you but to educate you. It is important for you to understand what is happening with your wife's body. If you are informed, it will help you help her through the slumps without taking her moods so personally. It's not something you can fix, but you can be an invaluable support for your wife. Just a hug and a few simple, understanding words can go a long way in smoothing out the rough roads of PMS.

HERE ARE FIVE THINGS YOU SHOULD NEVER SAY TO YOUR WIFE DURING PMS:

1. Why are you always so emotional? Can't you just get over it?

2. You know you should lay off the sweets.

3. You're the only woman I know who has these emotional outbursts.

4. If your relationship with the Lord was where it needed to be, then you wouldn't struggle with all this so much.

5. I think we need to check into getting you an exorcist.

HERE ARE FIVE GOOD THINGS TO SAY TO YOUR WIFE DURING PMS:

1. Honey, I love you. No matter what, I love you.

2. Is there anything I can do to make it better?

3. I think you deserve some time alone; let me put the kids to bed.

4. Even when you're sad, you're still beautiful.

5. Let's go get some ice cream!

HOME IMPROVEMENT—*Learn your wife's cycle and her unique responses to each season. Ask her to help you mark your calendar with the approximate dates of her next couple of cycles.*

 THOUGHT FOR THE DAY—*Every husband needs to know that when the hormones are flying and his wife has lost it—grab hold of her, hug her, and say I love you.*
—*LINDA [ST. LOUIS]*

CHAPTER 24

WHEN A WIFE IS HARDEST TO LOVE, SHE NEEDS IT MOST

Women are complex emotional creatures. Your wife doesn't need you to completely understand her or figure out all her ins and outs and ups and downs. She may not even understand these things about herself. But to seek to love her, no matter what, is a goal worth pursuing. Cindy of Princeville gave great wisdom in her survey response. She said, "If I'm crying, hug me. If I'm laughing, hug me. If I'm doing the dishes, hug me. If I turn away from your hug, especially then, hug me!"

When a wife is hardest to love, chances are this is when she needs it the most. When I was trying to explain this to Art, I knew I needed a word picture to help him understand. As I thought about what example I could use to help him get what I was saying, I decided to compare my emotional needs to his sexual needs.

Sex—now this is something most husbands understand. At least they understand their need for sexual intimacy on a consistent basis. I know that if I am not meeting Art's intimate needs, he's more likely to be tempted in this area. If Art is not meeting my emotional needs, then I am more likely to be tempted in the emotional area. I am likely to struggle with insecurity and doubt in the authenticity of his love, if he is not making an effort to fill me emotionally. Granted, my ultimate significance comes in my relationship with the Lord, but as Art needs me sexually, I need him emotionally.

This is where the dilemma often occurs. By the time I am emotionally needy, I am usually hard to love. I need Art to fill me emotionally like my physical body needs to be filled with food. If I feed my body on a consistent basis, then I have energy and I feel able to function. If, however, I starve my physical body, then I feel cranky, lethargic, and unable to exert energy.

Think about how you feel when it has been too long since you and your wife connected sexually. This is how she feels when it has been too long since the two of you have connected emotionally. She will be starving emotionally and likely exhibit the same symptoms I described when a body is starved for food. She'll be cranky and a little hard to love. But this is when she needs your love the most.

Ephesians 5:25–27 says, "Husbands, love your wives, just as Christ loved the church and gave himself up for her to make her holy, cleansing her by the washing with water through the word, and to present her to himself as a radiant church, without stain or wrinkle or any other blemish, but holy and blameless." Just before these verses Paul (author of this book of the Bible) tells wives to obey their husbands (verse 22). The *NIV Life Application Study Bible* says this in the commentary on these verses:

> Paul devotes twice as many words to telling husbands to love their wives as to telling wives to submit to their

husbands. How should a man love his wife? (1) He should be willing to sacrifice everything for her. (2) He should make her well-being of primary importance. (3) He should care for her as he cares for his own body. No wife needs to fear submitting to a man who treats her in this way.[1]

Christ loves the church with "agape" love. This is pure, unconditional love. It is a love based on the decision that no matter what, be she sweet or be she cranky, you choose to love her. This love pursues its bride. This love actively seeks to know how to love her. This love gives and does even when it's tired and doesn't feel like giving or doing. This is the love that drove Christ to do what He did for the church, even unto death. This is how God calls a husband to love his wife.

Kay Arthur, in her book *A Marriage Without Regrets*, writes:

> And how did Jesus love the church?
>
> He humbled Himself, girded on a towel and washed filthy feet, that she might be "cleansed by the washing of water with the word."
>
> He offered His flesh to be torn by evil men, that she might be without "spot or wrinkle or any such thing."
>
> He died on a cruel cross, that she might be made holy and blameless.
>
> O, beloved, our Lord loves us warts and all! Unconditionally, sacrificially, patiently, enduringly, and endearingly. God forgives and does not forsake. Read the gospels and see Him in action; read the epistles and see Him explained. Then you will know how a husband is to

love his wife. . . . Can you imagine what would happen throughout the homes of America if husbands would begin to love their wives in this *agape* way? Can you picture what would happen to the divorce rate? It would plummet like the stock market did in the Great Depression—only instead of depression the greatest boom this nation has ever known would arise.[2]

Easy? Not at all. Worth the effort? Absolutely. There will be days when loving your wife will be easy. There will be days when loving her takes every ounce of courage and strength. Let me leave you with the words the Lord gave to Joshua as he was about to lead the Israelites into the Promised Land. He too was overwhelmed. He too felt inadequate. Maybe just like you. But he was successful because he kept these words of his God close to his warrior heart: "Have I not commanded you? Be strong and courageous. Do not be terrified; do not be discouraged, for the LORD your God will be with you wherever you go" (Joshua 1:9).

HOME IMPROVEMENT—*Read Joshua chapter 1 and record your thoughts here.*

THOUGHT FOR THE DAY—*I can do everything through him who gives me strength.*—*[PHILIPPIANS 4:13]*

BE STRONG AND COURAGEOUS

T he other day I was going through paperwork tucked in forgotten files when I came across an old class address list from the newly married Sunday school class Art and I attended when we first got married. I glanced at the list, first recalling happy times and funny memories. I remembered the time we all got together and played our own version of *The Newlywed Game*. Then there was the time we went on a beach retreat and acted like kids at the miniature golf tourist trap. And how could I forget the popular "sex talk" given by our teacher, a gynecologist, every year around Valentine's Day. Then as I continued through the names, my mood became somber as I realized how many of the couples were no longer together.

Our class who had bonded during those early years and all set out on this marriage adventure together had fallen prey to statistics we are all too familiar with. Some had gotten shipwrecked because of financial troubles and others career pressures and failures. There were affairs both heterosexual and even homosexual. A tragedy of broken hearts, broken homes, and broken lives. Husbands were hurt, wives were hurt, and even more disturbing, small children were hurt.

I couldn't judge any of these couples, as sad as their stories made me, because but for the grace of God and our determined commitment to Him, Art and I could have been one of those tragedies. Marriage is hard. At times we all have felt ours is harder than most. And oh, how luring divorce seems at times—the ability to walk away from all the struggle and strife and chalk up our decision to the judicial system's politically correct term: "irreconcilable differences." Yet, to betray our commitment to one another and our covenant to God is to miss out on one of life's most precious blessings: a marriage.

We know we want our marriage to work, but at times we don't know how to make sense of it all. There are gender differences and personality differences. We have differing needs in differing degrees with differing expectations. What started out as simple love has grown increasingly complex and confusing. I know this, because I've lived it firsthand.

The last thing I desired in writing this book was to throw more information your way. We live in a culture where we are overloaded with information. Most husbands are familiar with the basics of marriage, but the thing I saw as missing was the inspiration to connect their heads with their hearts. To balance some fresh insights with inspiring stories that drive the central message home; to remind you that your marriage is worth it, so keep on keeping on.

My prayer for you in having read this message is that you will look at your wife in a new and exciting way. I hope something you've read has touched your heart and stirred your soul, making you fall in love with her all over again. As you venture on from here, rest assured that you've got what it takes to be the hero and capture her heart. ■

NOTES

CHAPTER 1
1. Dr. Robert McQuilken as quoted in Richard Exley, *The Making of a Man* (Tulsa: Honor Books, 1993).

CHAPTER 2
1. Prayer written by Elaine Hardt, copyright 2000. Used by permission.

CHAPTER 3
1. Quote from a Family Life Marriage Conference, "A Weekend to Remember." To inquire call: 1-800-FL-TODAY or visit www.familylife.com.

CHAPTER 4
1. Reprinted with permission from Ragan Communications, 1-800-878-5331.

CHAPTER 5
1. Patrick Morley, *What Husbands Wish Their Wives Knew About Men* (Grand Rapids Zondervan, 1998), 22.
2. Ibid., 25.

CHAPTER 7
1. Christin Ditchfield, "A Match Made in Heaven." N.1 *Power for Living*, 28 January 2001, 2–6. Used by permission of the author.
2. Dr. James Dobson as quoted by Joyce Landorf, *The Fragrance of Beauty* (Wheaton: Victor 1973)
3. Dr. James Dobson, *What Wives Wish Their Husbands Knew About Women* (Wheaton: Tyndale, 1975), 36.

CHAPTER 8

1. Holly Faith Phillips, *What Does She Want from Me Anyway?* (Grand Rapids Zondervan, 1997), 12.

CHAPTER 9

1. Beth Moore, *Breaking Free* (Nashville: Broadman & Holman, 2000), 196.
2. *NIV Life Application Study Bible* (Wheaton and Grand Rapids: Tyndale and Zondervan, 1988), 2166.

CHAPTER 10

1. Bill and Pam Farrel, *Men Are Like Waffles, Women Are Like Spaghetti* (Eugene Ore.: Harvest House, 2001), 11–12. Used by permission.
2. Ibid., 13.

CHAPTER 11

1. Dr. Ed Wheat, *Love Life for Every Married Couple* (Grand Rapids: Zondervan, 1980), 111.
2. Ibid.

CHAPTER 12

1. Gary Smalley, *If Only He Knew* (Grand Rapids: Zondervan, 1979).

CHAPTER 13

1. Lysa TerKeurst and Sharon Jaynes, *Seven Life Principles for Every Woman* (Chicago: Moody, 2001), 199–200.

CHAPTER 15

1. Patrick Morley, *What Husbands Wish Their Wives Knew About Men* (Grand Rapids: Zondervan, 1998), 166.

CHAPTER 16

1. "Johnny Lingo's Eight-Cow Wife" by Patricia McGerr. © 1965 by Patricia McGerr. First published in Woman's Day. Used with permission of Curtis Brown, Ltd.

CHAPTER 17
1. John Eldridge, *Wild at Heart* (Nashville: Thomas Nelson, 2001), 16–17.
2. Ibid.

CHAPTER 18
1. Gary Smalley, *If Only He Knew* (Grand Rapids: Zondervan, 1979), 119.
2. John Eldridge, *Wild at Heart* (Nashville: Thomas Nelson, 2001), 189.

CHAPTER 19
1. Dennis Rainey, *Lonely Husbands, Lonely Wives* (Dallas: Word, 1989), 255.
2. Linda Dillow and Lorraine Pintus, *Intimate Issues* (Colorado Springs: Waterbrook, 1999), 45.

CHAPTER 20
1. Dr. James and Shirley Dobson, *Night Light* (Sisters, Ore: Multnomah, 2000), 107.

CHAPTER 23
1. Niels H. Laursen and Eileen Stukane, *Premenstrual Syndrome and You* (New York; Fireside Books, 1983).
2. Jean Lush with Pam Vredevelt, *Women and Stress* (Grand Rapids: Revell, 1992), 108.

CHAPTER 24
1. *NIV Life Application Study Bible* (Wheaton: Tyndale and Grand Rapids: Zondervan, 1988), 2140.
2. Kay Arthur, *A Marriage Without Regrets* (Eugene Ore.: Harvest House, 2000), 65–67.

Art and Lysa TerKeurst are available for

marriage conferences and seminars.

To inquire about booking them together

for a speaking engagement or to

inquire about having Lysa speak to

your group, contact:

Proverbs 31 Ministries

PO Box 17155

Charlotte, NC 28227

1-877-731-4663

http://www.proverbs31.org/

or e-mail: office@Proverbs31.org

ABOUT PROVERBS 31 MINISTRIES

Proverbs 31 Ministries is a nondenominational organization dedicated to glorifying God by touching women's hearts to build godly homes. Through Jesus Christ, we shed light on God's distinctive design for women and the great responsibilities we have been given. With Proverbs 31:10–31 as a guide, we encourage and equip women to practice living out their faith as wives, mothers, friends, and neighbors.

What began in 1992 as a monthly newsletter has now grown into a multifaceted ministry reaching women across the country and around the globe. Each aspect of the ministry seeks to equip women in the Seven Principles of *The Proverbs 31 Woman.*

1. The Proverbs 31 woman reveres Jesus Christ as Lord of her life and pursues an ongoing, personal relationship with Him.

2. The Proverbs 31 woman loves, honors, and respects her husband as the leader of the home.

3. The Proverbs 31 woman nurtures her children and believes that motherhood is a high calling with the responsibility of shaping and molding the children who will one day define who we are as a community and a nation.

4. The Proverbs 31 woman is a disciplined and industrious keeper of the home who creates a warm and loving environment for her family and friends.

5. The Proverbs 31 woman contributes to the financial well-being of her household by being a faithful steward of the time and money God has entrusted to her.

6. The Proverbs 31 woman speaks with wisdom and faithful instruction as she mentors and supports other women and develops godly friendships.

7. The Proverbs 31 woman shares the love of Christ by extending her hands to help with the needs in the community.

MINISTRY FEATURES

NEWSLETTER—The Proverbs 31 Woman is a twelve-page, monthly publication, which is a storehouse of inspiration and information to equip women in the seven principles of the Proverbs 31 woman.

RADIO MINISTRY—The Proverbs 31 Radio Ministry airs a daily two-minute program heard on approximately four hundred networks across the country and overseas.

SPEAKING MINISTRY—The Proverbs 31 Ministry features

dynamic speakers who share life-changing and inspirational messages at women's conferences, banquets, and retreats.

ON-LINE SUPPORT GROUP—Through the Internet, this support group includes an on-line Bible study and book club for women who may not otherwise have an opportunity for fellowship.

ENCOURAGEMENT GROUPS—Women in churches around the country enjoy the benefits of small group Bible study and fellowship at their church, home, or office. These groups are chartered through Proverbs 31 Ministry.

SHE SPEAKS—Proverbs 31 Ministries offers training and certification for women to become Proverbs 31 speakers. If God has called you to the podium, call us!

For a sample issue of our newsletter, or more information on the ministry, write or call:

The Proverbs 31 Ministry
PO Box 17155
Charlotte, NC 28227

PROVERBS · 31
M I N I S T R I E S

877-p31-home (877-731-4663)
web site: www.proverbs31.org

Moody Press, a ministry of Moody Bible Institute,

is designed for education, evangelization, and edification.

If we may assist you in knowing more about Christ

and the Christian life, please write us without obligation:

Moody Press, c/o MLM, Chicago, Illinois 60610.

CAPTURE HER HEART

EIGHT-WEEK
STUDY GROUP QUESTIONS

This book can be used as material for a men's group study. Whether you are in a small accountability group or a larger men's Bible study group, *Capture Her Heart* will aid in helpful discussions as you learn together to make your marriage all God intends it to be. It is crucial that everything discussed within this group be held in the strictest of confidence. This group exists to encourage one another in the pursuit of godly marriages and to lift one another up in prayer.

YOUR WIFE NEEDS YOU TO BE THE SPIRITUAL LEADER OF YOUR HOME
Chapters 1–3

1. How did Dr. McQuilken's story inspire you?

2. What are some ways to be like Jesus to your wife?

3. Why is it important to pray for your wife? How could doing this improve your marriage?

4. Discuss this quote from chapter 3, "She needs a man who will not fight her but fight the fire-breathing beast who seeks to destroy you both."

5. How can you make sure to put on your spiritual armor every day?

6. Which home improvement had the most impact on your wife this week?

YOUR WIFE NEEDS YOU TO BE HER TEAMMATE IN RAISING THE KIDS AND TAKING CARE OF THE HOME
Chapters 4–6

1. First Peter 3:7 says, "Husbands, in the same way be considerate as you live with your wives." Discuss ways to be more considerate of your wife.

2. What are some creative ways to thank your wife for all she does?

3. Describe the parent you longed for as a child. How can you become this for your children?

4. What are some things only you can give to your children as their father?

5. What does it mean to be your family's provider?

6. Which home improvement had the most impact on your wife this week?

YOUR WIFE NEEDS YOU TO TREAT HER LIKE A PRINCESS
Chapters 7–9

1. How could you help build your wife's self-esteem?

2. How can you make your love more obvious to your wife?

3. Discuss Bill McCartney's quote about the effectiveness of a man's life being determined by the countenance of his wife.

4. How can you learn to focus more on your wife's positive qualities?

5. How can you "let the peace of Christ rule in your heart" as Colossians 3 instructs?

6. Which home improvement had the most impact on your wife this week?

YOUR WIFE NEEDS YOU TO COMMUNICATE WITH HER
Chapters 10–12

1. How can you make the communication differences between you and your wife work to enhance and not harm your relationship?

2. How can you make Ephesians 4:29 come alive in your marriage?

3. If you only had one more conversation with your wife, what would you say? How can you say these things to her on a regular basis?

4. What is the key to understanding a woman's "hints"?

5. Why is persistence important to a marriage? How can you continue to be encouraged to press on?

6. Which home improvement had the most impact on your wife this week?

YOUR WIFE NEEDS HER FRIENDS AND NEEDS YOU TO ALLOW HER TIME WITH THE GIRLS, BUT ULTIMATELY SHE WANTS YOU TO BE HER BEST FRIEND
Chapters 13–15

1. Why is it important for your wife to have time to develop friendships with other women?

2. What are some creative ways for you to allow her time with the girls?

3. How can you help your wife find her "me"?

4. Why is your belief and support of her dreams so important?

5. What are some things you and your wife can do to nurture your friendship?

6. Which home improvement had the most impact on your wife this week?

YOUR WIFE NEEDS YOU TO BE A "TRIPLE A" ENCOURAGER BY GIVING HER APPRECIATION, AFFIRMATION, AND ADMIRATION
Chapters 16–18

1. How does it affect you to know your wife is in the process of becoming what you think about her?

2. How can you delight in your wife?

3. What could you be in the habit of doing that makes your wife feel extraordinary and rare?

4. Why is it important to ask your wife where she feels vulnerable and then seek to help and protect her in those areas?

5. What are some ways to make your wife feel appreciated?

6. Which home improvement had the most impact on your wife this week?

YOUR WIFE NEEDS TO FEEL EMOTIONALLY FILLED BEFORE SHE DESIRES TO BE SEXUALLY INVOLVED

Chapters 19–21

1. How do men and women approach the marriage bed differently?

2. Comment on this quote: "If you make your wife priority number one behind God and if she feels secure in that, your needs will be met."

3. What is the difference between having sex and making love?

4. Do you know of some quaint, romantic, getaway places where you could take your wife for a retreat together? Share ideas of places with each other.

5. How can you get behind the eyes of your wife and see life as she does? How could this improve your romantic life?

6. Which home improvement had the most impact on your wife this week?

YOUR WIFE NEEDS YOU TO UNDERSTAND
THAT THERE ARE SOME THINGS YOU
WILL NEVER UNDERSTAND. THIS DOESN'T
MAKE EITHER OF YOU RIGHT OR
WRONG—JUST DIFFERENT
Chapters 22–24

1. How did the "Just Because" story inspire you?

2. What are some ways to help your wife through the struggles of PMS?

3. Are there other things you would add to the list of things to say or not to say to your wife during particularly emotional times?

4. How does Jesus inspire you to love your wife?

5. How does Joshua 1:9 encourage you? In what ways can you draw strength from the Lord to love your wife unconditionally?

6. Which home improvement had the most impact on your wife this week?

FOCUS ON THE FAMILY.

Welcome to the Family!

Whether you received this book as a gift, borrowed it from
a friend, or purchased it yourself, we're glad you read it! It's just
one of the many helpful, insightful, and encouraging
resources produced by Focus on the Family.

In fact, that's what Focus on the Family is all about—providing inspiration, information, and biblically based advice to people in all stages of life.

It began in 1977 with the vision of one man, Dr. James Dobson, a licensed
psychologist and author of 16 best-selling books on marriage, parenting,
and family. Alarmed by the societal, political, and economic pressures
that were threatening the existence of the American family, Dr. Dobson
founded Focus on the Family with one employee—an assistant—
and a once-a-week radio broadcast, aired on only 36 stations.

Now an international organization, Focus on the Family is dedicated
to preserving Judeo-Christian values and strengthening the family
through more than 70 different ministries, including eight separate
daily radio broadcasts; television public service announcements;
10 publications; and a steady series of books and award-winning
films and videos for people of all ages and interests.

Recognizing the needs of, as well as the sacrifices and important
contributions made by, such diverse groups as educators, physicians,
attorneys, crisis pregnancy center staff, and single parents,
Focus on the Family offers specific outreaches to uphold and
minister to these individuals, too. And it's all done for one purpose,
and one purpose only: to encourage and strengthen individuals
and families through the life-changing message of Jesus Christ.

• • •

For more information about the ministry, or if we can be of help to your
family, simply write to Focus on the Family, Colorado Springs, CO 80995
or call 1-800-A-FAMILY (1-800-232-6459). Friends in Canada may write
Focus on the Family, P.O. Box 9800, Stn. Terminal, Vancouver, B.C. V6B 4G3.
or call 1-800-661-9800. Visit our Web site—www.family.org—
to learn more about Focus on the Family or to find out if
there is an associate office in your country.

We'd love to hear from you!

Other Faith and Family Strengtheners
From Focus on the Family ®

The Marriage Masterpiece takes a fresh appraisal of the exquisite design God has for a man and woman. Explaining the reasons why this union is meant to last a lifetime, it also shows how God's relationship with humanity is the model for marriage. Rediscover the beauty and worth of marriage in a new light with this thoughtful, creative book. A helpful study guide is included for group discussion. Available in hardcover and two-cassette album.

Learning to Live With the Love of Your Life— an encouraging and insightful book that offers practical guidelines for enhancing intimacy, communication and romance in your relationship. For both newlyweds and longtime mates, it's a powerful plan for holding on to the wonder and joy of love. Request it for yourself or as a gift for a couple you love. Available in hardcover and two-cassette album.

• • •

Look for these special books in your Christian bookstore or request a copy by calling 1-800-A-FAMILY (1-800-232-6459). Friends in Canada may write Focus on the Family, P.O. Box 9800, Stn. Terminal, Vancouver, B.C. V6B 4G3 or call 1-800-661-9800.

Visit our Web site (www.family.org) to learn more about the ministry or find out if there is a Focus on the Family office in your country.